Creative Essence

Creative

Cleveland's Sense of Place

Essence

Nina Freedlander Gibans

The Kent State University Press   Kent and London

This publication was made possible in part through the generous support of Barbara P. Ruhlman.

Frontis: South facade of the Cleveland Museum of Art. Photograph by Jennie Jones.

Designed by Christine Brooks and set in 10.5/14 Minion. Printed on 157 gsm Japanese enamel stock by Everbest Printing Co. Ltd. of Hong Kong.

Most photographs of works of art reproduced in this volume have been provided by the owners or custodians of the works and are reproduced with their permission.

LIBRARY OF CONGRESS CATALOGING-IN-PUBLICATION DATA
Gibans, Nina Freedlander.
    Creative essence : Cleveland's sense of place / Nina Freedlander Gibans.
        p.   cm.
    Includes index.
    ISBN 0-87338-819-4 (alk. paper) ∞
    1. Art, American—Ohio—Cleveland Region—19th century. 2. Art, American—Ohio—Cleveland Region—20th century. I Title.

    N6535.C6G53 2005
    709'.771'32—dc22   2004065758

British Library Cataloging-in-Publication data are available.

SEEING SONGS by Nina Freedlander Gibans
(setting: Laufkuff's Bookstore, ca. 1930)

"Art should be as spontaneous as the song of a bird."—William Sommer
" . . . forms (are) more beautiful because they were never meant to be beautiful . . ."—Margaret Bourke-White

I.
Suspended and arched over riverways
"bridges hold the songs!"
Hart Crane told Bill Sommer at the bookstore
where they finished yesterday's sentences today,
"I see them in black and white," Bourke-White broke in.
"City forms are beautiful because they were never meant for beauty."

Boat horns and whistles, the song of this city
bridges strong as rock salt beneath the riverbed,
mills gorging tree sites keep blooming and dying.
Blooming and dying with the work seasons,
Alleluia!

Smokestacks sang work songs triumphantly,
city painters saw smoke wisps or clouds,
trees *were* there before the stacks;
green, then gray and brown-dung sadness
Lamentations.

II.
"Painting calls me to the country," spoke Bill
where the sun shifts gears in an afternoon
greenlands turn to reds and bronze.
I travel with the painter
fifteen miles east of the riverbed
ten miles south or to the west
a stone's throw from the painter eye
standing in the grasses picking color for my song.
Hallelujah!

III.
Bill could *hear* in color; Margaret came to sing along.
We sing again as he had sung.
I know I hear Hart's
words in color.
Amen.

Contents

Dedication

On my first visit to Kent as a candidate for the position of director of the Urban Design Center, I was nervous about my inevitable meeting with Foster Armstrong, the founding director of the UDC whom I was hoping to replace. Just how gracious could anyone be to a potential successor with an agenda for change? But as I struggled to shake off my West Coast jet lag over toast and coffee at our breakfast interview, I quickly realized that I was the one whose grace was at issue.

Foster welcomed me to Ohio as an old friend and long-time collaborator whose ideas he valued and went out of his way to nurture, like an eclectic gardener who finds room for every kind of flower and revels in the melange of their collective blooming. In the two years we spent together at the UDC before his death, I saw that this was his way with everyone: his students and faculty colleagues, the neighborhood residents and community groups he served, members of the design profession and other nonprofit organizations he supported. I have never seen anyone so delighted by the successes of others or more committed to unlocking the vast opportunity he saw in the people and places of northeast Ohio.

The Creative Essence: 1900–2000 series was enriched by Foster's deep appreciation for the achievements and potential of our region and his determination to engage us all in a celebration of who we are, where we came from, and what we can be. This book and the dialogues on which it is based are dedicated to the spirit of critical enquiry and optimism that he brought to the project and to everyone who had the privilege of working with him throughout his life.

RUTH DURACK
Director, Urban Design Center of Northeast Ohio

Foreword

For over a century the cultural life of Cleveland has emerged from the character of its New England founders, from the industrial base rooted in eastern European traditions, and from the heritage of its African American population arriving from the South. With Indian trade paths giving way to a powerful commercial hub, Cleveland became defined as a leading cultural center civilized by its parks and beautifully developed neighborhoods. The crowning identifier has been the quality of its cultural organizations, a source of life and inspiration for artists.

The teachers and students attracted to the Cleveland Institute of Art, formerly the Cleveland School of Art, created a specific character in Cleveland within the broader regionalist and arts and crafts trends that emerged in the earlier years of the twentieth century. The flourishing of a fine tradition of watercolor, painting, sculpture, graphic arts, textiles, ceramics, enamels, and jewelry were a direct result of the strength of its faculty. The remarkable achievements of artists in industrial design reflected both the New England belief in the well-made object and the exhilaration from the highly successful industrial environment that stimulated faculty and students. The cultural environment in which artists prospered included the gifts and legacies of proud industrialists who created the cultural giants that are the pride of the city today: the Cleveland Museum of Art and the Cleveland Orchestra, the artistic and musical proving grounds of the Cleveland Institute of Art, the Cleveland Institute of Music, and the Music School Settlement, all of which are located in the context of Case Western Reserve University and the University Circle. The cultural priorities of Clevelanders have nurtured artists, bringing them together not only with the inspiring cultural context but also with patrons and supporters.

This publication captures for Cleveland both the broad sense of self and the details of the Cleveland artists. The value that is placed upon the past in this volume gives direction for the present and the future. As we experience the diversity of artistic endeavors—and as we try to address a tidal wave of information from our present day world culture—it is vital that we understand what is distinctive about Cleveland both in its broader culture and among artists. We are all indebted to Nina Gibans for her remarkable effort to provide this written history.

KATHARINE LEE REID
Director, Cleveland Museum of Art

Preface and Acknowledgments

In nearly forty years of being an administrator, writer, teacher, researcher, participant, advocate, and observer in one location, it seemed the right moment to pull together what I know as an art historian, have experienced as the manager of arts projects, and have used in coordinating complex projects. So when the Cleveland Artists Foundation asked me to head a lecture series, I knew it had to be something different, provocative, even visionary. I know the people of the arts scene. I have worked with many of them for years on arts budgets, percent for art laws, creating art and architecture, public art projects, and forums. My husband and I have visited local institutions and galleries as a matter of daily life. My students have studied in these places, and winced and smiled as they encountered the new. I have coordinated major studies in the museum world, coproduced prize-winning videos for public television, and worked with artists closely. It was the right time.

Between January 27 and 30, 2000, a visit from consultant Susan Szenasy, editor of *Metropolis* magazine, spurred the Cleveland Artists Foundation to enter into a process of examining the "creative essence" of the region by developing dialogues among groups of regional specialists and academicians, leaders of cultural institutions, and artists and architects to determine the ways in which this area's creativity is distinguished and distinctive. This format followed many months of discussion and development and involved the cooperation of many persons and institutions (see Appendix D). I am most grateful to the board, Lecture Committee, and staff of the Cleveland Artists Foundation; the Ohio Arts Council; the Thomas F. Peterson Foundation; and most particularly Barbara P. Ruhlman, for her belief in and support of this effort.

The Cleveland Artists Foundation developed through the series' sessions discussions about the significant stories of the art created in the Cleveland area during the twentieth century. The subjects included our regional sense of place, people, and industry; the library as a cultural center for art and architecture; the galleries and contemporary art; our man-made environment; the historical perspective; the artists' perspectives; and the role of the museums. Over the following fourteen months, I organized the stories into coherent forms, managed the information, and related the information to the national and global contexts.

Dialogues took place at many different venues in and around Cleveland, including at the Western Reserve Historical Society, the Cleveland Museum of Art, the Sarah Benedict House (Cleveland Restoration Society), the Cleveland Center for Contemporary Art (now the Museum of Contemporary Art, Cleveland), the Cleveland Institute of Art, and the Cleveland Public Library. Cleveland's public radio station 90.3WCPN ideastream broadcast the programs live and invited listener questions and opinions and, as did WCLV 104.9, placed the full text on its website. Those who guided our media networking were not only advisers but welcome critics and questioners. We thank David Kanzeg, program director of 90.3WCPN/NPR, for allowing us to replace the two-hour, prime-rime favorite *Fresh Air with Terri Gross* six times, keeping the faith that we could measure up to broadcast standards. Thanks to Bob Conrad, executive of WCLV, for pushing us toward the Internet, archiving and preserving our work. Thanks to Carol Bosley, coordinator of Educational Services, and Mark Rosenberger, Gary Manke, and their crews for their involvement as advisers and coproducers of the WVIZ/PBS ideastream program. This video program comprises the DVD included with this book. Senior production staff members Mark Rosenberger of WVIZ/PBS ideastream and Jesse Epstein of CINECRAFT, Inc., helped create the video *Creative Essence,* which was selected for inclusion in the twenty-seventh Cleveland International Film Festival in 2003. The series has broadened the use of technology and media for dialogue within the community, established multiple ways of promoting cultural affairs, and expanded community participation in cultural programming. The Cleveland Artists Foundation owes thanks to many people in an effort such as this.

The community participants numbered in the dozens. They started, continued, and expanded the dialogue. The audience questioners and radio callers with good queries and ideas raised important issues. The conservative guess is that 20,000 listened to each radio broadcast and that another several hundred have listened to the archived programs on WCLV.

I thank the Martha Holden Jennings Foundation for the grant that allowed me to transform the materials from this book into curriculum units that can be used by teachers of art and history in the study of this region. This valuable site is available as a permanent community resource at www.clevelandartandhistory.org.

There are those who helped with the planning and concept behind this publication. Foster Armstrong saw its form before it had substance. Richard Karberg and William Busta added many ideas and contributions of visual material, and the collectors of regional work generously donated and lent their photographs of art objects. William Busta, Anthony Hiti, Richard Karberg, Barbara Megery, and Susan Leggett critiqued individual chapters or the whole of this book. Rachel Wayne Nelson worked through the chronology and proofread, and Linda Harris typed up the entries and all of the lists. Rotraud Sackerlotsky, Jane Tesso, William Busta, and Robert Hanson assisted with different aspects in the preparation of the manuscript.

A publication such as this one is nothing without the visual material to make it real. Thanks to everyone who photographed works of art, dug into their own treasure trove of slides, turned over undefined works on walls, identified works of art, helped find artists who are not here now, and gave permission to use artwork. You are the wonderful network of folks who are very important to any regional project.

I am grateful to those persons and institutions that became supporters of the publication through their generous contributions of time and by absorbing all or some of the costs of creating such a publication. It was special fun encountering collections new to me such as that of Ernest Bohn, whose collection of WPA prints is in Special Collections at Case Western Reserve University, and to work with persons such as Monica Wolf at the Cleveland Museum of Art, who had studied with some of the artists. We found mutual interest in stories and perspectives.

In the beginning, the several dimensions of getting the messages to folks who listen, read, relisten, and reread the ideas of the project seem like distant goals. For me this was part of the vision: addressing the ways in which people absorb ideas and information. Thus the live dialogues, the video production, the publication, and the website were part of a whole delivering material in multiple ways. One is not always exactly sure how that will happen. My belief is that it is necessary in a world of multiplicity and complexity. Thank goodness for the believers along the way.

The content for this book comes from many sources, as clarified in the notes, but special homage should be given to the Cleveland Arts Prize initiated by the Women's City Club forty years ago. Their visual arts and architecture committees have identified distinguished visual artists and architects in our midst. That distillation (though not the only guidepost by any means) served me well as I considered all of the "voices" that needed to be heard.

I have especially valued the wisdom and experience of Joanna Hildebrand Craig, the Kent State University Press's excellent editor-in-chief, whose steadfast devotion to making this the best book possible endured throughout.

I am grateful always to an ever-ready supporter for any of the above activities and for those related to this publication—my husband, Jim, an architect and ally in all things related to our region's cultural life. I am blessed by his patience and wisdom. Tangling with these issues over a lifetime has enriched our life enormously.

Beginnings

In his wonderful book *Seasoning: A Poet's Year,* David Young finds the connectedness in Ohio between place and being. For those of us who have lived and worked in northeastern Ohio over the better part of the twentieth century, or even less, he resonates those special characteristics that have kept us here all of these years—close to our roots, close to the soil, close to the industry, close to things that matter about this place.

> Northern Ohio, where I live, feels like nowhere in particular. It's part of the Great Lakes bioregion, and nobody knows whether it is the Middle West or the East or something in-between. . . . My part of the world lacks the features of landscape—mountains, sea cliffs, waterfalls, deep forests, rugged outcrops, sweeping vistas—that we tend to associate with significant natural beauty. . . .
>
> In a way, though, this uncelebrated part of the world is exactly right. . . . I want to show that time and place can reward you in the quotidian, the everyday, that you need not go to any place other than the unremarkable place where you happen to find a daily, weekly, monthly beauty in your relation to time and the environment.[1]

Ohioans know his sentiments are true. South Woodland Road in the spring, the Chagrin River in the summer, the Cleveland MetroParks' "emerald necklace" in the fall, and the riverfront in the Flats or lakefront in Bratenahl in the winter are all places of common beauty in this region.

Those of us who enjoy deep pleasure in living in this "in-between" find it to be a place in which we live and work, grow and mature, launch and be launched, and travel away from and back to. We have lived and worked elsewhere, but this is home. In showing people this region, we spin tales about the roads to Akron or

1

Wooster most traveled, the trips over the bridges of the Cuyahoga from East to West Side, the winding river and the wide-open lake, the drive to the country to get corn, the arching lilac trees over Martin Luther King Boulevard at Euclid Avenue, trips downtown. For many Clevelanders, the cultural institutions are just as significant to their impression of the area. The Cleveland Museum of Art is a "second home," and we have sat rapt in Severance Hall. We relish in the unparalleled scenic architectural beauty of the inner-ring suburbs and marvel at the lift and the jack-knife bridges over the Cuyahoga.

Just as David Young, poet, has taught me to see a new Ohio, the region's artists give me new insight about their world of seeing and feeling. These artists give us the eyes to look at our environment. Using charcoal, pen and ink, cameras, or watercolors to record raw data in sketchbooks, on film, and on paper, they have provided their perspectives of our neighborhoods, our urban landscapes, and our surrounding countrysides. They have seen the ways in which the corners of fences connect; city, bridges, and water come together; and waterways become home for birds and broken shapes. They know our light and landscape and find it forever interesting. They live and work among us and remind us of what it feels like to live here. They travel for renewal, and because they want to connect to a wider world, but many call this part of the world home, even though there have never been enough opportunities to exhibit or enough patrons to sustain their art careers. They are the soul of the region.

Our Regional Culture: Place, People, and Industry

Various regions of the United States have distinct characteristics. When the South is mentioned, we envision a particular culture and way of life and think of certain architectural designs unique to Georgia and Alabama or geographical features particular to the Carolinas. The American West, New England, the Pacific Northwest, and other regions also have had little trouble articulating what is unique about their part of the country. The area that tends to be the most difficult to describe, however, has been the Midwest. Perhaps this is because this large and variously defined region seems so central to what we think of as "normal" and "regular" and "typical" in the American experience.

Our artistic identity is similarly vague. In William H. Gerdts's book on regional art, *Art across America,* only fourteen pages out of a thousand are devoted to northeast Ohio. Even when this region is mentioned, Gerdts only points out that "art developed much more slowly [there] than in the rest of the state."[1] No published work really helps us understand our identity. What exactly *is* this region, its boundaries and makeup? What is particular, distinctive, different about where we live?

To answer this question we have to examine northeastern Ohio through its place, people, and industry—the way our natural resources give us distinction and build our industrial base and how our European heritage provides clues about who we were and are. We are a blue-collar region, born of the soil and its materials. A tough city. Early we were leaders in working with the oil, steel, rubber, and polymers, and we manipulated the materials and design for industries here and everywhere.

Like artist Charles Burchfield, who eloquently wrote many times and in many ways about this region, many people have trouble with the word "regionalism" because it implies that regional work is provincial. However, if we understand that one can live and work in one locality and still reach out to the art of the whole world, we find comfort in our sense of place. In order to gain that sense, reflect on it, and verbalize or articulate it in one's creative effort, we must experience it at its core. We must stay the course long enough to absorb the best and the worst: the lakescape, the landscape, the topography, the feel of the country and city, the sound of it, the language, the look of green fields and brown fields, and, finally, the community.

Place

We rely on the great journals of Lewis and Clark for the definitive story of the West in the early 1800s. Artists such as George Catlin recorded in oil, charcoal, and watercolor the native life in the 1830s along the Missouri River at a last moment of these people's great splendor, and we can never forget those indelible portraits. In the same way, the Hudson River School artists painted portraits of the Northeast's landscapes at an important moment when we were reexamining our ideas about nature.

The early story of our region begins with the region's first residents, the various tribes that lived along the banks of the Cuyhoga. Documentation of this history began in earnest in the 1840s with the work of Charles Whittlesey, a skilled writer who owned and edited the *Cleveland Daily Gazette* and the *Cleveland Herald and Gazette* prior to becoming the area's primary geologist. Whittlesey participated in or led the first geological and archaeological surveys in the state, during which he explored and documented ancient Indian earthworks throughout Ohio. Over time, Indian settlements were discovered as villages grew into towns and cities and as roads and highways were carved out of the bluffs and banks along the Cuyahoga. Many of the main roads in Cleveland, including Euclid Avenue and Woodhill and Detroit Roads, are built over old Indian trails. A bronze plaque on the National City Bank building at 107 St. at Euclid Avenue (the former site of the Western Reserve Historical Society) marks this: "At this point two important Indian paths intersected—the Lakeshore Path leading from Presque Isle (Erie, Pennsylvania) to Detroit, Michigan and the Mahoning Path leading from Lake Erie to the Great Salt Springs near Niles, Ohio." Cleveland was also the meeting of the Portage Trail and the Buffalo Trail.[2]

Frank Wilcox, noted painter, printmaker, watercolorist, and teacher, wrote and illustrated *Ohio Indian Trails* (1933) and *The Ohio Canals* (1967), which preserves these trails, canals, and our heritage. Unlike George Catlin, however, Wilcox never saw or met any of the Indians he includes in his illustrations of his research into and documentation of the early history of the canals—their development, routes, engineering, and construction. His placement of native figures into the natural settings is based on his extensive historical and archaeological research and keen artistic observation of the region.

Plaque on the National City Bank (once the site of the Western Reserve Historical Society) indicating the intersection of the Lakeshore Path and Mahoning Path going east and west.

The Ohio Canal Corridor, running north to south, was a trade path used by the region's native people for thousands of years. In the Cuyahoga River valley they lived on abundant supplies of fish and plants and large game. Western settlers began displacing the seasonal Indian population after the War of 1812, when this fertile valley was recognized as an important place for industrialization. The mouth of the Cuyahoga River became the northern terminus of the Ohio & Erie Canal, which extended south to the Ohio River at Portsmouth and provided a "superhighway" for the transportation of food, manufactured goods, raw materials, and crops. After the Cuyahoga Valley Line Railroad was completed in the 1880s, people and goods could travel easily throughout the area, and trade goods from as far away as the Gulf of Mexico were able to make their way to Cleveland.[3]

In a project undertaken to define the regional identity of northeast Ohio in a most unique way, the Ohio & Erie Canal Association has been archiving the many natural, historic, cultural, and even industrial resources of a linear landscape that

Frank Wilcox, *Twilight*, ca. 1932, watercolor, 18" x 22". Courtesy of Elaine and Joseph Kisvardai. Photograph by Berni Rich.

Frank Wilcox, *Along Canal Street, Cleveland*, ca. 1960, zinc plate etching. Courtesy of Elaine and Joseph Kisvardai. Photograph by Berni Rich.

starts at Cleveland's lakefront and follows the course of the old Ohio Canal, all the way through Zoar to New Philadelphia. One of the aims of this Ohio & Erie Canal National Heritage Corridor project is to reestablish the links among Cleveland, Akron, Canton, Massillon, and New Philadelphia that existed when transportation was mainly conducted along the canal. The project also hopes to gain a better understanding of how people settled this area.

While the Hudson River School of American artists was producing many of the mid-nineteenth-century landscapes, this kind of painting had not really caught on all over the country. Before there were nurturing institutions and a social context for valuing fine arts, artists positioned their work to sell—to serve clients who wanted portraits or paintings for prestige—and painted genre paintings on subjects symbolic of personal or communal importance, including townscapes and

Above left: August Biehle, *View of Canal,* ca. 1940, oil on canvas, 31½" x 38¼". Courtesy of the Janet Alder Family. Photograph by Berni Rich.

Above right: August Biehle, *Overgrown Hermitage Along Road to Zoar,* ca. 1920, gouache and pencil, 18" x 24". Courtesy of the Janet Alder Family. Photograph by Berni Rich.

Left: George C. Adomeit, *Farm Landscape–Ohio,* 1899, oil on canvas, 9" x 12". Courtesy of the Shoreby Club. Photograph by William Pinter.

George C. Adomeit, *Chagrin Valley,* ca. 1940, oil on canvas board, 16" x 20". Courtesy of the Shoreby Club. Photograph by William Pinter.

paintings of the battles on Lake Erie. There are few examples of landscapes from that early time. The first landscape, produced in the 1860s, was probably done for Harvey Rice, father of Ohio Free Public Schools, who owned the Kingsbury Run land depicted in the painting. During that transitional period, the paintings offered some visual comment on the artists' state of mind about the lot of the unskilled laborer, the rich client, or their ambivalence about the changing city.[4]

Painting as a fine art started in earnest in the region in the 1870s. Inspired by the French Impressionist out-of-doors subjects, regional artists of this period searched for similar scenes and found them in the woodlands, valleys, and waterways of Ohio. Those we know best came out of the summer schools that started as early as 1885 with Otto Bacher's retreat in Richfield and, in 1896, F. C. Gottwald's at Zoar, the picturesque communal village along the Tuscarawas River. These pioneers were students of Archibald Willard, painter of *The Spirit of '76* and an arts leader. Gottwald was one of the first central figures in the early Cleveland art scene. Through the early twentieth century, August Biehle was one of several artists who explored and painted the countryside around Zoar and Berlin Heights, near Sandusky, and Frank Wilcox's watercolors of the countryside outside of Cleveland captured the charm of the old houses in the village and the hilly farm land surrounding them. From these paintings we get a sense of the life of these nineteenth-century people, their homes and their work places.[5]

From 1903 to 1915 popular Cleveland School of Art teacher Henry Keller (self-described as "recently from Dusseldorf, Munich, and Paris") invited peers and

Above left: August Biehle, *Berlin Heights Farmhouse*, ca. 1920s, oil on canvas, 26" x 34". Courtesy of Hahn Loeser & Parks LLP.

Above right: Frank Wilcox, *The General Store*, ca. 1930, watercolor, pencil, and gouache on paper, 21½" x 29¼". Courtesy of Hahn Loeser & Parks LLP.

Left: Henry Keller, *The William Lee Farm, Berlin Heights*, 1915, oil on board, 20" x 14". Courtesy of Cleveland Artists Foundation, gift of Karl Humm.

students to his family farm in Berlin, near Sandusky, not only to paint the countryside but to freely explore style and color in ways not yet possible in the confines of an art school curriculum of the time. Assignments led students to examine the wheat fields, weathered houses, trees, old doorways, barns, Lake Erie beaches and surf.[6]

Right: Clara Deike, *The Willow,* 1910, oil, 16" x 20". Courtesy of Richard A. Zellner.

Below left: William Sommer, *Bach Chord,* 1923, oil on board, 20" x 23¾". Courtesy of Akron Art Museum, gift of Russell Munn in memory of Helen G. Munn.

Below right: William Sommer, *Yellow Cows,* 1941, watercolor and graphite, 19" x 23½". Courtesy of Joseph M. Erdelac.

Similarly, around 1914 William Sommer, congenial and popular in the artists' community, offered camaraderie and philosophical dialogue among artists, poets, and musicians at his studio in a converted schoolhouse at Brandywine (at the edge of what is now the Cuyahoga Valley National Park), a venture that proved to be ongoing and long lived. And George Adomeit, busy working in calligraphy and establishing a printing business, always found time to explore the countryside as well.

Art depicting this natural environment is abundant. Others whose works record walks and explorations include Charles Burchfield, who took walks and painting trips with his mentor Henry Keller, and Paul Travis, who for forty years was one of the most popular teachers at the Cleveland School of Art. These same artists and others traveled widely to examine American scenery, notably in the East at such artist enclaves as Provincetown, Massachusetts, and Monhegan Isle, off the coast of Maine, but returned home to this region's beautiful landscape.

While many of these artists painted appealing scenes of beaches and coves, and while there had long

Top: Charles Burchfield, *Retreat of Winter,* 1937, watercolor, 11" x 17". Courtesy of Jay and Kathy Ferrari. Photograph by William Pinter.

Bottom: Paul Travis, *Summers Harvest,* ca. 1917, watercolor, 18" x 22". Courtesy of Elaine and Joseph Kisvardai. Photograph by Berni Rich.

Holly Morrison, *Facing North*, 1995–96, gelatin silver print photograph, 40" x 40". Courtesy of Federal Reserve Bank of Cleveland.

been pictures documenting the history and maritime life of the lake—ships carrying people and cargo, battle scenes—there were no artists at the time who explored the lake environment. It wasn't until the last decades of the twentieth century that Erie's endless cool gray, its pollution, its mystery was studied in drawings, photographs, and paintings. Perhaps Lake Erie as a subject was seldom used as landscape material because there are no far shores to focus on. Photographer Holly Morrison said, "Visible or not, Lake Erie is part of our everyday life. With its moisture and reflective surface, the lake creates a unique light that particularly casts our colors. It affects our sense of space, opening a distant horizon that offers possibilities beyond the limited viewscapes of our gentle hills."[7]

People

The earliest record of Ohio Indian life comes from the *Jesuit Relations* (1656–57), a series of letters and accounts from Jesuit priests coming to America to teach the Indians about Catholicism. In this region they found more than thirty native villages. When the first explorers and settlers moved into the Ohio Country in the seventeenth and eighteenth centuries, the Ottawa, Wyandot, Mingo, Miami, Delaware, and Shawnee tribes had already left an indelible mark on Ohio's artistic and cultural heritage. An example of an artifact of particular beauty is the pipe tomahawk with silver inlay that was given to Thomas Worthington by Shawnee chief Tecumseh in 1807.[8]

After the opening of the Northwest Territory in 1787, European settlers found new homes here in earnest. In the fifty years after 1800, the population increased from 45,000 to more than 2 million.[9] Ohio's position between the Ohio River, as the southern boundary of the Old Northwest, and near the extremely important Great Lakes to the north made it a main thoroughfare to the West, South, and North.

Migrants came primarily from New England, the mid-Atlantic, and upland South. Those from New England settled in the Connecticut Western Reserve, Marietta, Putnam, Granville, and Worthington. Cultural characteristics from these settlers include towns laid out with central greens and commons, Greek Revival–style buildings, and Protestant religious institutions. The largest number of settlers came from the mid-Atlantic region. Those large numbers that came from bordering Pennsylvania were mainly German and Scots-Irish, and they settled in the middle of the state. Strong German influences can be seen in the sturdy log cabin and barn constructions and the pious religious sects. Southern migrants coming from Virginia, mostly Scots-Irish and Presbyterian, settled in the west-central part of the state, where larger farms and long brick houses with double porches were characteristic.

Europeans, most from Germany, can be counted among the settlers in the early part of the nineteenth century. Many came to the large Ohio cities, Cleveland and Cincinnati, but they also settled in the Scioto and Miami valleys and in Auglaize, Stark, and Tuscarawas Counties. Accounting for 22 percent of the pre-1850 immigrants were the Irish, who came to escape the potato famines afflicting Ireland and for greater economic opportunities.[10] Although drawn to the large centers, these migrants capitalized on employment opportunities in the railroad and canal industries, such as in Cleveland's Flats, where the Ohio & Erie Canal terminated, bringing lumber, coal, and other raw materials via the Mississippi and Ohio Rivers. Immigrants arriving to dig canals and work the docks built shanties on the hillsides along the Flats and eventually moved to the Ohio City area. And by the 1850s the Tremont area had become an ideal location for immigrants from Germany, Poland, Russia, Greece, and Syria who came to work in the steel mills at the base of the hills. But as the immigrants began moving into the city's neighborhoods, the wealthy industrialists began moving out—into grand homes on Euclid Avenue, known as Millionaires' Row, or into the West Side areas bordering the city.

During the last part of the nineteenth century, growing economic opportunities in Ohio, and in Cleveland in particular, saw the population grow to new heights and new diversity. New immigrants came from Eastern and Southern Europe, making Cleveland home to large numbers of Slovaks, Hungarians, Italians, Russians, and Poles. By the turn of the century, 75 percent of Cleveland's population was either foreign born or first generation. In the early decades of the twentieth century, African Americans began migrating north to Cleveland, 70,000 by 1930 and 235,000 by the 1990s. Midcentury the city welcomed large numbers of non-European migrants who came to work in the steel mills in Lorain. Changing immigration laws through the century, easier ocean travel and land transportation, the city's economic position, and international situations had a tremendous impact on the region's immigration patterns. Beginning in the later decades of the twentieth century, immigrants from China, Korea, Vietnam, India, Mexico, Central America, and even Appalachia added to the diversity of the city.[11]

But it was the German immigrants who had perhaps the most significant impact on the cultural life of the city. Immigrant Otto Bacher, the first internationally known Cleveland painter, applied painting inscriptions on commercial ves-

Frederick C. Gottwald, *Cleveland Market,* ca. 1895, oil on canvas, 13⅛" x 18¼". Courtesy of Federal Reserve Bank, Cleveland.

August Biehle, *Tug on the Cuyahoga*, 1932, lithograph, 8" x 12". Courtesy of Cleveland Artists Foundation, gift of Frederick and Helen Biehle.

sels. Similarly, painter August Biehle apprenticed with his father, who produced decorative murals for the homes of Cleveland's industrial entrepreneurs.[12] George Adomeit, known mostly as a prolific painter and printmaker, cofounded the Caxton Company, which gained wide renown as a fine engraving and commercial art firm. Louis Rorimer, the son of a German immigrant who became successful in the tobacco business, made considerable contributions to the arts in Cleveland partly through his teaching at the Cleveland School of Art but primarily as head of the Rorimer-Brooks Company, which brought artists and artisans together to serve discerning clients who demanded the finest craftsmanship in design and furnishing. And Martin Rose, who emigrated to the United States from Hungary by way of Vienna, seeking better opportunities to use his training, established the century-old Rose Iron Works, designers of ornamental works in iron, aluminum, copper, alloys, and glass for stores, homes, restaurants, public buildings, and institutions.

During the 1880s and 1890s, those who had a vested interest in seeing this area develop culturally were wealthy and politically powerful, and they wanted civic and cultural institutions that reflected their vision of grandeur and elegance. And so the waterways between Europe and America were busy not only with immigration but with travel by those whose wealth and interests allowed them to emulate in America the splendor of the European culture. This was the Gilded Age, the "robber baron" era of elegance and craftsmanship. The reflection of this vision extended out of their travels and Continental tastes to their churches and homes, now icons of that era.

One such industrial leader was Jeptha H. Wade, founder of Western Union. Owner of farmland and natural woodland that became a public park in 1872 (encompassing most of University Circle) and president of the Lakeview Cemetery Association, Wade was a leader in the development of a range of enterprises and institutions: a bank and savings and loan that were predecessors of the Huntington Bank, the Euclid Avenue Opera House, Case School of Applied Sciences, and the American Steel and Wire Division of U.S. Steel. However, it is the artwork he collected on the Wade family's wide, international travels that reflects his and their personal and cultural interests. Wade's appreciation for great art was evident in his grandson Jeptha Wade II's donations to the newly opened Cleveland Museum of Art (CMA) in 1916: his family's Claude Monet oil painting *Gardener's Cottage;* an oil sketch by John Constable, *Hamstead Heath, Looking toward Harrow;* the Puvis de Chavannes; and, among other items, two Pacific Northwest Tlingit daggars with abalone, bone, and other inlay as well as an African knife. And after the museum opened the Wades continued to donate or underwrite acquisitions for the

Masumi Hayashi, *Cleveland Cultural Gardens,* 1987, panoramic photo collage, 39' x 61", Kodak paper. Courtesy of the artist.

collection. Another hero of Cleveland's cultural institutions is industrialist Leonard Hanna. Of his bequests, CMA director Katharine Reid says, "I find it hard to choose from the many riches that he either acquired for himself and bequested in 1958 or funded as direct purchases. . . . Everyone's favorite, and mine too, is the purchase of the Picasso *La Vie*."

We also turn to the public spaces as reflections of the region's immigrant aspiration and industrial past. Lakeview Cemetery is a burial place for more than 100,000 people, regardless of race, religion, or economic status, and it pays homage to Cleveland's history and tells its stories in stone, mosaic, and glass. Modeled after the great garden cemeteries of Victorian England, France, and the eastern United States, Lakeview was built by Italian gardeners and stonecutters who settled in the city and built their community on the hills nearby. Rockefeller Park, donated to the city by industrialist John D. Rockefeller, features the Cultural Gardens—landscaped gardens and statuary honoring Cleveland's many ethnic communities. Beginning in 1927, Hebrew, Italian, German, Lithuanian, Ukranian, Slovak, Polish, Hungarian, Czech, Yugoslav, Russian, Irish, Greek, Syrian, Romanian, Estonian, African American, Chinese, Finnish, Indian, and Vietnamese gardens are among those established along the East Boulevard and Martin Luther King corridor. Oversight for preservation and restoration for the park rests with the Cleveland Cultural Garden Federation, which represents the diversity of the garden groups' descendents.

Industry

This region is the epitome of the industrial Midwest, a concept that was just crystallizing at the turn of the twentieth century and connected Cleveland, Lorain, Ashtabula, Chicago, and Milwaukee. The importance of the waterways and an abundant supply of raw materials to industry cannot be overstated. This region had both.

The first "business" in Cleveland, opened in 1801, when Cleveland's population totaled seven, was a distillery. By the time the Ohio & Erie Canal was completed in 1832, there was a bank, a newspaper, a marketplace, and a temperance society. By midcentury there were railroads, and the Civil War years saw a demand for the region's iron and steel products. By the turn of the twentieth century, the Standard Oil Company, Sherwin Williams Company, Lake steamer service between Buffalo and Cleveland, the Winton Motor Carriage Company, and other automobile manufacturers (two being Peerless and Stearns) were operating out of Cleveland. Between 1892 and 1932 there were 111 automobile manufacturers in Cleveland. Manufacturing; machine tooling; coal, steel, and oil shipping; and shipbuilding and manufacturing made this area prosperous and amassed vast fortunes for the industries' founders, many of whom modeled their industrial development after

"A New Cleveland Trade Empire," *Cleveland Plain Dealer,* June 29, 1930. Reprinted with permission of the *Plain Dealer*.

workable industrial forms found mainly in England. They brought their aesthetic ideas and the craftspeople to execute them from central Europe and other parts of the world in which they traveled. By 1920 the city ranked fifth in the manufacture of paints and varnishes, printer's presses, and electric batteries. Cleveland ranked second in the manufacturing of women's ready-to-wear clothing and was a nineteenth-century American fashion center.[13]

Along with the entrepreneurial spirit came a desire for offices and residences that reflected the expectations of those industrial leaders. We feel the lasting effects of the founders and leaders—the Mathers, Wades, Rockefellers, and Van Sweringens—who saw and seized the opportunities and whose civic vision and taste for European fine craftsmanship set the tone for the inner-ring suburban living and accompanying services. They supported the development of our cultural institutions, adapting elegant Continental styles—gleaned from their travels abroad—for their homes and workplaces. People who could handcraft furniture and hand-block and hand-stencil wallpaper were valued, and so clients of companies like furniture maker Rorimer-Brooks could depend on receiving high-quality designs based on European and American styles and idioms.

The alliance of arts and crafts occurred as artists, designers, and artisans found themselves working in the commercial world in order to make a living. Similarly, this region's industrial base itself served as creative inspiration, with many taking their cues from the milieu, looking at the materials and landscapes and manipulating them. It was out of this environment, for example, that the Cleveland Institute of Art's (CIA) Industrial Design program was born in 1930. During the Great Depression, when many artists were without means of making a living, the CIA Industrial Design program, led by Viktor Schreckengost, helped artists find new areas of practice in commerce and industry.

The Region's Man-Made Environment

Determining what has been distinctive and distinguished in a region's architecture is not an easy task. As local architect Richard Fleischman said during one of the community dialogues, "Defining space is a tremendous responsibility. We can go to the symphony on Thursday, Friday, and Saturday and we can all be critics. We can go to the opera and fill the State Theater and be critics in the opera, but how many of us can walk into a building with the same kind of enthusiasm and understand and criticize the building as an idea. . . . We're taught music, we're taught theater, but we are way behind in trying to teach architectural space."[1] But what criteria should one use for architectural distinction? For one urban planner, distinction is in the impact of highway systems and urban renewal. For another architect, distinction is in the Frank Gehry building on the Case Western Reserve University campus or in the great homes that once lined Euclid Avenue.

The look of a community—a city, a public square, an avenue—can be distinguished by good design or undistinguished by mediocrity. The former may be harder to achieve but easier to recognize. In architecture there is something inherently right in certain proportions of windows to wall space or in the allocations of space and materials. One can be architecturally illiterate and still "feel" the perfection. For many of us, Cleveland's architects have created something that feels like home.

Over the last one hundred years, there have been three distinct periods in the development of our city, beginning with Tom Johnson, Cleveland's mayor during the first decade of the century, whose progressive spirit is reflected in the Group Plan for the city's public buildings. Organized around a mall inspired by the Mall in Washington, D.C., then under construction, the Burnham Plan was to be a "gateway" leading down to a grand railroad station (never built) on the lakefront. Seven public buildings—including the Federal Court House and Custom House,

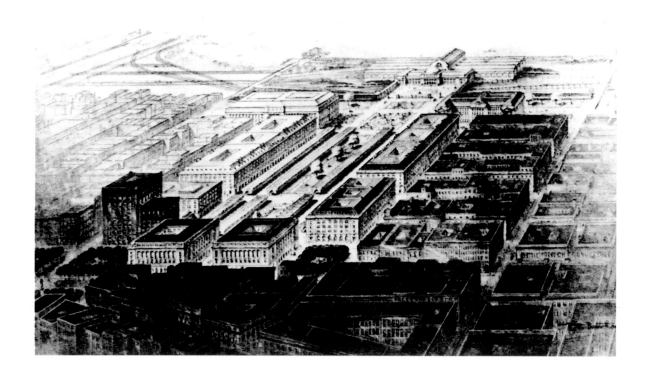

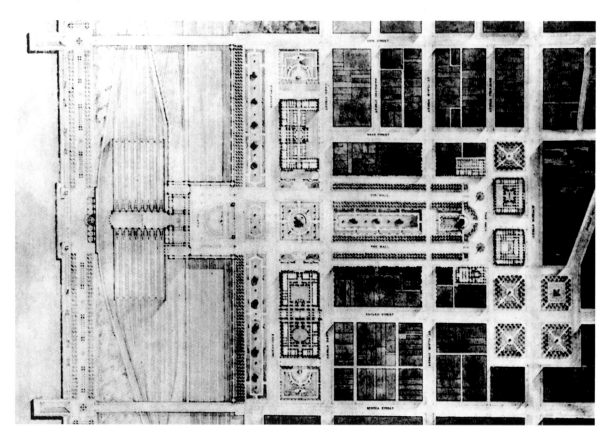

the Cleveland Public Library, and the Cleveland Board of Education—were designed in beaux arts and second Renaissance modes, executed in stone, and similarly scaled so as to create a unified look and feel.[2]

The next major period of development took place in 1925–26 when the Van Sweringen brothers persuaded the city to allow the development of their Rapid Transit from downtown to what was to become Shaker Heights. Their intent was to connect with downtown the land they had bought and intended to develop. They wanted to give wealthy Clevelanders the option of moving to the suburbs, as the immigrants filled the city, as well as a means of escaping industrial pollution. Their community concept included schools, golf courses, and appropriate architecture—usually in colonial, English, or French styles—as well as a retail development designed in an octagon and inspired by eighteenth-century European royal squares. Shaker Square was the second shopping center built in America. In its day, this plan was considered pioneering and regarded as a brilliant vision of national stature.

In 1960 the Erieview Plan emerged, reflecting a period of national urban renewal that sought to clear out all the old, decrepit buildings to establish a new

Facing page: The Burnham Plan, 1903, a bird's-eye perspective, looking north. Below: Plan view.

Above: Jennie Jones, *Skyline of Public Square*, 1992.

urban vision. The Erieview Plan intended to renew what had become a tacky, gap-toothed 9th Street by replacing older buildings, poorly maintained and believed to be of little civic importance, replacing our legacy with the largely undistinguished office buildings and parking lots that now line the street. Currently, Cleveland is seeing the results of the 1990–2000 Civic Vision plan designed to revitalize the city's downtown and lakefront and beyond.[3]

On Landmarks and the City

Landmarks define the character of the city. Cleveland was conceived as the capital of the Western Reserve territory; the Connecticut Land Company selected our site, where the Cuyahoga River and Lake Erie meet, and planned for grand avenues and a public square. Our city's distinguished public buildings, with their tough midwestern exteriors, have withstood the test of time, and our historic religious buildings have been recognized as magnificent works of art. The many beautiful homes in Lakewood, Cleveland Heights, and Shaker Heights, as well as our historic theaters, arcades, and banking halls, have made the region rich with architectural landmarks.

Shoreby House, 1890. Charles Schweinfurth, architect. Samuel Mather, industrialist client. Photograph by Jennie Jones.

Peter van Dijk, architect of Blossom Music Center, tells his story about coming to Cleveland in 1961 as a young architect.

I soon realized that there were many other magnificent buildings from the early part of this century . . . and that we had a cadre of really wonderful architects here. . . . Many of them were cultured gentlemen who had gone to the beaux arts and were very well-educated people. The two that rose up above all of them . . . were Charles Schweinfurth and J. Milton Dyer, complete opposites working at the same time in our history. I liked to compare them to the two famous architects working in Rome at the 17th century.

Borromini, who was in with the Pope and all the well-to-do, got the wealthy projects. Bramante was sort of a real Bohemian character and he got the low-budget jobs. Both of them were geniuses and both were doing magnificent work, one with a huge budget and one with a little budget. And I feel the same way about Charles Schweinfurth. He was a brilliant architect and he got the jobs like the Union Club, Trinity Cathedral, the Mather Building at Case Western Reserve University, whereas Dyer got the Cleveland Athletic Club, and City Hall. J. Milton Dyer's life really spanned from his early work, City Hall, and his late work, the Coast Guard station. Dyer talked about space and timelessness; Schweinfurth talked about decoration. Dyer's buildings are all very classical, very special, and very eclectic.[4]

While Cleveland's architecture historically reflected styles seen elsewhere, rather than invented here, it was well designed in comfortable idioms, and there was much to be proud of. Unfortunately, most of the earliest architecture has not survived, and we willfully destroyed some of the more substantial later examples, like the mansions on Millionaires' Row. But in more enlightened recent years, since 1971, we have tried to preserve districts and the best and most important buildings by assigning a "Landmark" designation that legislates design review before alteration. Examples include land owned by John D. Rockefeller in East Cleveland and Euclid

Left: St. Theodosius Cathedral, Main Onion Spire with Three Lower Spires, 1911–33, Starkweather Avenue. Frederick Baird, architect. Photograph by Jennie Jones.

Right: The Temple, 1923–24, 1958, East 105th at Ansel Road. Charles R. Greco, architect. Photograph by Jennie Jones.

Golf in Cleveland Heights, which were translated into prime properties for gra-cious living. In the latter, developer Barton R. Deming employed Garden City prin-ciples and deed restrictions, while architects Howell and Thomas, Charles Schneider, and others designed homes that resulted in Fairmount Boulevard becoming known as "the Euclid Avenue of the Heights." The diversity of the nearly two dozen His-toric Districts in the city serves as homage to our history and development. The first such designation was Hessler Road and Hessler Court, located within Univer-sity Circle, with its neoclassical and bungalow character, with a trace of Norman, Tudor, and Swiss chalet styles, and 1870s wooden block pavement. Other Historic Districts include Ohio City, the city's oldest independent community, 1836–54; Franklin Circle, a residential community featuring mid-to-late-nineteenth-century styles; and Market Square, the commercial area near the West Side Market.[5]

The Warszawa Neighborhood Historic District is the core of the Polish neigh-borhood, where simple homes with dormers, oriel windows, and recessed porches remind us of the Queen Anne style elements used in the architecture of the time. Here St. Stanislaus Church stands in pristine glory. In 1891, when it was originally built by a Polish congregation in the tradition of medieval gothic churches, St.

Easter Sunday, St. Stanislaus Roman Catholic Church, Forman Avenue at East 65th Street. Photograph by Bog-den Pieniak.

Stanislaus was the largest Gothic-style church in the country west of New York City's St. Patrick's Cathedral. In 1998 major restoration renewed the locally made red brick and dressed stone on the exterior. The conservation specialists researched and restored multicolored stenciling to the walls and ceiling and followed the pastel color palette as they worked on walls, ceiling, columns, woodwork, and plaster ribs to reconstruct the interior in all of its original majesty. Other churches and temples are equally noteworthy. St. Theodosius Russian Orthodox Church Cathedral, with its twelve domes (representing Christ and his Apostles), a traditional design, is furnished with a chandelier from Czechoslovakia and an icon screen from Kiev. And The Temple, near University Circle, is a neo-Byzantine design reflective of Hagia Sophia. What we borrowed we made distinctive, our own.[6]

Architects and Architectural Firms

The region's architectural history starts before the 1870s and leaves a legacy of classic Greek Revival, Roman, Renaissance, and French empire styles and medieval, Romanesque, and Gothic revivals scattered across the landscape. The ma-

Left: Federal Reserve Bank, 1923, Superior Avenue at East 6th Street. Walker and Weeks, architects. van Dijk Pace Westlake, restoration architects. Photograph by Jennie Jones.

Right: Society for Savings Building, 1889–90, 127 Public Square. Burnham and Root, architects. Corner lamp restoration, 1992. van Dijk, Johnson and Partners, restoration architects. Photograph by Jennie Jones.

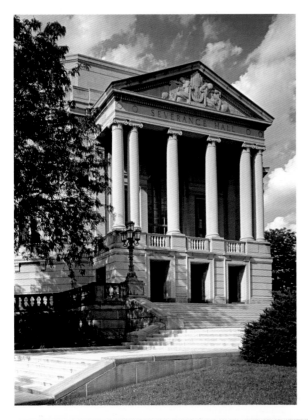

Above left: Severance Hall, 1931, Euclid Avenue at University Circle. Walker and Weeks, architects. Photograph by Roger Mastroinni.

Above right: Hope Memorial (Lorain-Carnegie) Bridge pylons, 1932. Frank Walker, architect. Wilbur J. Watson, engineer. Henry Hering, sculptor. The 43-foot-high pylons feature replicas of transportation vehicles: covered wagon, hay wagon, stagecoach, automobile, and trucks.

Left: Detail, Federal Court House (Old Federal Building), gilded ceiling, 1905–11, 201 Superior Avenue NE. Arnold W. Brunner, architect. Photograph by Jennie Jones.

The Region's Man-Made Environment   29

Schweinfurth House, 1894, East 75th Street between Chester and Euclid Avenues. Charles F. Schweinfurth, architect. Photograph by Jennie Jones.

jority of builders were not so skilled, but there were skilled designers and builders, such as Charles Heard and Simeon Porter, who built some of the region's most important public buildings, and Jonathan Goldsmith, builder of the most beautiful of the Western Reserve's Greek Revival houses.

Following the 1893 Chicago World's Fair, where famous New York and Chicago architects designed a model city to show a maturing America how we, too, could have elegant, classically designed cities, Cleveland became the first to apply these plans to its growing cityscape. City leaders brought Daniel Burnham here to design a Group Plan that would give a defining structure to our downtown and a strong form out of which to grow and expand.

The Group Plan called for beaux arts buildings to line the Mall. A significant contributor to this collection of eclectic, classical buildings was the Cleveland firm of Walker and Weeks, two young architects who trained under Louis Sullivan in Chicago. The firm designed the original Cleveland Public Library, the Public Auditorium, the Board of Education building, and the Federal Reserve Bank. Perhaps their finest contribution is Severance Hall, arguably one of the most beautiful concert halls in the world.

Above: Blossom Music Center, pavilion and lawn, 1968. Shafer Flynn van Dijk and Associates, architects. Peter van Dijk, design architect. Photograph by Bruce Kiefer.

Left: The Nathan and Fanny Shafran Planetarium, Cleveland Museum of Natural History, 2002. van Dijk, Pace Westlake, architects. Paul Westlake, design architect. Photograph by Nick Merrick, Hedrich Blessing.

Cleveland's creative leanings in architecture have always reflected the conservative character of the city. Yet there are many exceptional buildings within the city and its suburbs, and there has been superb preservation—some of the finest anywhere: "Cleveland's buildings represent the full range of types one would expect to find in an American city shaped by industry and commerce over the past two centuries. . . . [The city] has shaped its own special quality, a feisty mix of urban toughness and suburban gracefulness."[7]

Following are profiles of some of the architects and firms, past and present, responsible for the "look" of the city, beginning with the oldest ongoing firm.

Abram Garfield (1872–1958) was the son of James A. Garfield, twentieth president of the United States. After studying at Williams, at MIT, and a year of travel abroad, Garfield returned here to open his architectural practice in 1897. His legacy is long and distinguished: from *Abram Garfield, Architect,* 1905–22, to *Westlake Reed Leskosky,* March 2004–present. Over its long history this firm's buildings include grand homes in Bratenahl and Shaker Heights, Eldred Hall on the Case Western Reserve campus, the John Hay Residence, Blossom Music Center, and the Nathan and Fanny Shafran Planetarium. The firm has also made its mark with exemplary major restorations of the Federal Reserve Bank building, the Huntington Bank building, and the Society Bank building. The aesthetic on which the firm gained its reputation is one of grace and elegance; shapes tend to be unusual yet classical, quiet rather than pushing space aggressively. Lead architects *Peter van Dijk* and *Paul Westlake* both received Cleveland Arts Prizes for their work. (See Appendix B.)

J. Milton Dyer (1870–1957) attended the École des Beaux-Arts in Paris at the turn of the century, returning home to Cleveland to start up his own architec-

Tower Press Building (Wooltex Factory), 1908, 1900 Superior Avenue. Robert D. Kohn, architect. Renovation 2003, Sandvick Architects, Inc.

Lakewood house (right) designed by Clarence Mack. Photograph by Al Teufen.

tural practice. Accomplishing his major work between 1900 and 1911, he excelled in all kinds of architecture—residential, ecclesiastical, industrial, and commercial. Some of his more outstanding projects, each different and distinctive, include the Tavern Club (1905), a private men's club designed with a gabled facade; Cleveland City Hall, with its classical beaux arts look to fit in with the 1903 Group Plan; and the later (1940) U.S. Coast Guard Station at the mouth of the Cuyahoga River, reflecting the influence of European modernism.

Frank Ray Walker (1877–1949) and *Harry E. Weeks* (1871–1935) were both educated at MIT. After travel and work elsewhere, they came to Cleveland in 1905 to take advantage of the opportunities here, especially in the realization of Burnham's Group Plan. Both men worked for J. Milton Dyer before opening their own firm in 1911. *Walker and Weeks* specialized in banking halls, completing sixty of them throughout Ohio, but in Cleveland became known for their commercial, public, cultural, and religious structures. Some of their well-known works include Severance Hall, Cleveland Municipal Stadium, Allen Memorial Medical Library, Cleveland Public Library (Main Branch), and the Federal Reserve Bank.

Charles F. Schweinfurth (1856–1919) designed some of Cleveland's most distinguished homes for the city's industrial leaders, including fifteen along Euclid Avenue, Cleveland's Millionaires' Row, between East 12th and East 40th Streets. (The only one still standing is the Samuel Mather house on the Cleveland State Univer-

Tudor House on Shaker
Lakes. Photograph by
Jennie Jones.

sity campus.) Other Schweinfurth residences include Mather's summer home in
Bratenahl, now the Shoreby Club. Trinity Cathedral and its Parish House at East
22nd Street and Euclid is thought to be his finest building, and the bridges over
Martin Luther King Drive are a favorite of many who pass under their broad
arches and honk to hear the echoes.

Benjamin Hubbell (1867–1953) and *W. Dominick Benes* (1857–1935) worked together from 1897 to 1935. Benes was Jephtha Wade's personal architect, and he
designed the Wade Memorial Chapel at Lakeview Cemetery, with its interior designed by Louis Comfort Tiffany as a memorial to the elder Wade. The grandson
commissioned the firm to create Cleveland's "Temple of Art and Culture," the
Cleveland Museum of Art, a classical revival building, and they developed plans
for Wade Park with the museum as its focus. In the early decades of the century,
Hubbell and Benes designed the West Side Market and had plans for developing a
public center there, and they created a number of important public structures
between 1905 and 1930, including the YMCA building and the Ohio Bell Tele-
phone building.

Robert D. Kohn (1870–1953), architect of the Tower Press building (formerly the Wooltex Factory), was one of eight firms that was asked to submit plans for the Cleveland Public Library building. Kohn was a forward-thinking and articulate proponent of a coherent philosophy of industrial architecture. He pled for an honest, dignified design for factories. The Wooltex/Tower Press building, recently renovated as a living-working space for artists, is an excellent example of reform architecture, which Kohn "built with the declared intention of creating pleasant surroundings for the workers, providing not only slow-burning construction of reinforced concrete, and proper ventilation and lighting, but a new artistic treatment. Instead of the usual fancy brick facing on the façade and the common brick on the back, common brick was used throughout, laid carefully with raked dark purple joints. . . . The workrooms were stenciled in a simple geometric weaving pattern in two flat colors at the tops of the columns and at the ends of the transverse steel girders. The result is a humane factory building."[8]

Clarence Mack (1888–1982) designed thirty-two houses in northern Ohio between 1914 and 1938, adapting established traditional exterior styles to the needs of his clients. He used classic proportions, symmetry, and entryways that brought the details of French eclectic style and Georgian architecture to these buildings. The interiors were equally carefully designed, elegant, and polished. Mack built fifteen houses on Lake Avenue in Lakewood and lived in many of them as he built

Shaker Square, ca. 1950s.
Courtesy of Coral Realty.

Lakeview Terrace, 1937.

them. He also built seven houses for the Van Sweringen brothers on South Park Boulevard and South Woodland Roads in Shaker Heights.

Phillip L. Small (1890–1963) and *Charles B. Rowley* (1890–1984) practiced architecture together from 1921 to 1928, during which time M. J. and O. P. Van Sweringen selected them to design one of the five demonstration homes for their development, Shaker Heights. Together they completed more than forty residences (Georgian and Tudor) there, as well as Daisy Hill Farm, the Van Sweringens' home in rural Hunting Valley. They designed the Cleveland Play House, a part of Moreland Courts, and Shaker Square.

Herman Gibans Fodor (HGF) was established in 1935 when *Joseph Weinberg* (1890–1977) joined with the firm of *Conrad and Teare* to design Lakeview Terrace, one of the first public housing projects in the country and a pioneer in the design of multifamily housing. Continuing this tradition, HGF also recently completed the comprehensive modernization of a major part of Outhwaite Homes, another historic Cleveland public housing estate, and is currently undertaking the design for the Lakeview Terrace renovation. Lewis Mumford, the illustrious architecture and social critic, used Lakeview Terrace as an example of a good plan for its placement of buildings, use of the terrain, abandonment of costly streets, and interior playground. This project was recognized as "one of the best public housing projects in the country" and "a milestone in the history of American architecture."[9]

Robert A. Little (b. 1915) studied under Marcel Breuer and Walter Gropius at Harvard University and came to Cleveland in 1945 seeking to apply the principles of the Bauhaus. His first major local commission in 1949 was the prize-winning Shaker Square branch of Halle's department store. He was recognized for the human scale of his work and especially known for creating homes that would enhance a family's quality of life, personified by the development of Pepper Ridge, the first planned street of truly modern homes in the Cleveland area. These homes were positioned for their landscape settings and customized to the owner's needs. Little was selected for the Cleveland Arts Prize in 1965 because of the excellence of his design work and for his role in introducing the "language and philosophy of modern architecture to Cleveland." He was ahead of his time in his energy-saving and environmentally sensitive features and believed that everyone could afford good design.

Robert P. Madison (b. 1923) forged his own distinguished path in education and training earning degrees, honors, and Fulbright Scholarships based on the strength of his work. Not only have important buildings been designed or renovated by *Robert P. Madison International,* but the firm, as well as its founder, has also served as a mentor for hundreds of young African American architects and engineers, many of whom have gone on to do their own distinguished work and establish other African American architectural firms. The firm has been involved in nearly every major downtown building project in the last decade, from the RTA stations on the waterfront line to the Langston Hughes Branch of the Cleveland Public Library (see Malcolm Brown) to the renovation of the Cleveland Public Library's Main Building.

Fred Toguchi Associates, formed in 1962 under the leadership of *Fred Toguchi* (1922–1982), is regarded as creating buildings in the region that are particularly hospitable to families and community cultural events, buildings such as the Beck Center for the Arts, the Mayfield Regional Library, the Ashtabula Arts Center, and undergraduate dorms at Case Western Reserve University. The Rosenfeld Home in Shaker Heights embraced its environment of gardens and emulated the clean lines and spaces that were characteristic of his work. Toguchi was a recipient of the Cleveland Arts Prize in 1965, and an annual memorial architectural lecture at Kent State University was established in his name.

Above: Ohio Aerospace Institute, south facade, 1993. Richard Fleischman & Architects.

Right: House in Shaker Heights, 1966. Don Hisaka, architect.

Don Hisaka (b. 1927) has designed buildings from Cleveland to Tokyo with a single focus: graceful and attractive no matter how commercial the setting or utilitarian the agenda. Beginning in 1960 when he opened his practice in Cleveland, he has designed buildings like Beachwood's Signature Square office complex, the glass atrium connecting Thwing and Hitchcock Halls at Case Western Reserve University, and the University Center at Cleveland State University with characteristic attention paid to the surroundings and their relationship to the building. The national award–winning home he designed for himself in Shaker Heights is carefully placed on a pie-shaped wedge of land that inspired a unique and simple design that combines successfully all the qualities of his buildings. He was awarded the Cleveland Arts Prize in 1970.

Richard Fleischman and Partners, founded in 1961, has been conceptualizing various projects over the past forty years and producing Cleveland's most cutting-edge architectural designs, led by *Richard Fleischman* (b. 1928) and his unique sense of modernism that is a fusion of innovation and available technology. Their designs include cultural institutions, educational facilities, and corporate headquarters.

Paul Volpe (b. 1961) served under Mayor George V. Voinovich as the city's commissioner of architecture from 1983 to 1989, helping plan and design more than $150 million worth of municipal projects. In 1989 Volpe founded *City Architecture, Inc.,* a firm that specializes in urban design and neighborhood revitalization. A strong advocate for sustainable, livable communities, Volpe has presented his views in numerous forums and expressed strong interest in providing cities with projects that create quality environments that successfully manage development and growth. The impact of City Architecture's "new urbanism" designs is just beginning to be recognized on the riverfront, in midtown, and in the inner-ring suburbs.

Art in Architecture

Beginning with the earliest cave paintings, man has adorned buildings and public spaces. Great civilizations decorated their buildings and their surroundings with sculpture, murals, mosaics, stained glass, tapestries, paintings, fountains, and gardens. These works are true portraits of earlier life and the culture that helped

Elmer Brown, *Freedom of Speech,* 1942 (restored 1990), oil on masonite, 8'10" x 21'. Courtesy of City Club of Cleveland.

Left: Edwin Mieczkowski, *Sommer's Sun,* 1978, oil on canvas tondo. Brett Memorial Hall, Main, Cleveland Public Library. Photograph by Peter Hastings.

Right: William Sommer, *The City in 1833,* 1934, mural. Brett Memorial Hall, Main, Cleveland Public Library. Photograph by Don Snyder.

shape our heritage. So too, we in northeast Ohio can trace our regional history, its diverse heritage and art styles, by looking at the sculpture or monuments in public squares, in front of buildings, in parks, and even in cemeteries. While the marriage of art and architecture really started with our beaux arts buildings, it's important to note that the incorporation of art into public architecture took a great leap forward during the Public Works Art Project (WPA), the 1933 government initiative that created a program to fund artists during the Great Depression.

The Cleveland Public Library is an excellent example of the use of art in public spaces. Sculpture, murals, tiles, and decorative arts are an integral part of the library's buildings and collections, using themes from classic to current times and featuring local artists. An early distinguished work in the library is directly opposite the main entrance; William Sommer's *The City in 1833* (1934) depicts Public Square as it might have looked early in Cleveland's history. In the second-floor lobby of the library's Main Branch, you can see the WPA mural painted in 1934 by Cleveland artist Donald Beyard. It depicts early transportation along Cleveland's waterfront in 1835.[10] In 1994 the library commissioned art for thirteen ceilings and walls in the Louis Stokes wing, continuing the tradition of nourishing all aspects of the human spirit.

The use of allied arts in Cleveland's early-century architecture furthered the notion of public art. Sculptures and murals adorn the Federal Reserve Bank and the old Courthouse; the sconces on the Board of Education building are beautiful and functional light fixtures. Craftsmanship is evident all over, around, and throughout our older buildings. Individual artists were hired to design for companies making architectural embellishments. The Rose family is one such example. The work of Rose Iron Works, which was founded in 1904, can be found throughout this region. The family company worked on ornamental design with architects Charles Schweinfurth, Walker and Weeks, J. Milton Dyer, and Garfield-Harris-Robinson and with interior designers like Rorimer-Brooks. Their work has been seen in a Halle Brothers Dress Salon Screen, at the restored Higbee Silver Grille, on the H. W. Beattie and Sons building, on a Cleveland Botanical Garden wall, and in the homes of such leading families as Samuel and William Mather, the Van Sweringens, and the Blossoms. When personal tastes shifted away from wrought ironwork during the 1950s and 1960s, the company produced a variety of ornamental pieces in diverse styles, such as signs of the zodiac for Cleveland Hopkins Airport and numerous other murals and corporate logos and other industrial metalworking. The company's work has received significant acclaim and been displayed in museums throughout the country, including the Cleveland Museum of Art, the Renwick Gallery of the Smithsonian Institution, and the Museum of Fine Arts in Boston.

Paul Fehér, for Rose Iron Works, *Art Deco Screen*, 1930, wrought iron and brass with silver and gold plating. Courtesy of Cleveland Museum of Art.

With the influence of European modernism following World War II, traditional craft elements disappeared from buildings and were replaced by long, clean white walls, squared ceilings, and unadorned facades. Any artwork that was used was commissioned or purchased for the walls, floors, and plazas. We yearn for the elegance, but the craftspeople are increasingly scarce and the traditional materials are increasingly expensive. Those restoring the older buildings know these realities only too well.

Preserving History and Moving On

Some of the most distinguished regional work of recent years has been in the area of restoration. The buildings and sites in Cleveland and surrounding areas attest to this and represent noteworthy examples of historic restoration (Terminal Tower, Cleveland Public Library), historic preservation (Playhouse Square Theaters, Shaker Square), and adaptive reuse (Lincoln Park Baths). The challenge is to be

Allen Theatre, 1921, C. Howard Crane, architects; restoration 1998, GSI Architects.

honest about the worthiness of the buildings in terms of who we were and are and what we hope to resonate about that in the preservation effort. Preservation is renewal; at its best, it also frees us to see the possibilities for the future.

The *Guide to Cleveland Architecture* explains in its introduction that the architecture of Cleveland reflects the end of a stylistic period rather than a beginning, citing the Terminal Tower (built in 1930) as an example because it reflects the culmination of the beaux arts style and marks the end of the 1920s. In the later half of the twentieth century, this region, like so many others, lost its architectural vision. Every so often distinctive buildings did appear—such as Blossom Music Center— but no real "concepts" came forth to capture our attention and sustain our excitement. In the 1960s there was an attempt to redevelop East 9th Street into a "people place." But the skating rink built at Erieview Plaza was never used; and, similarly, the Galleria shopping mall, developed later at this edge of business traffic, was unable to compete successfully with the Tower City conversion to a shopping mall in the 1980s and with suburban commercial development. And like so many other cities, Cleveland sprawled further and further east and west. We demolished what remained of the Euclid Avenue mansions and allowed huge corporate megastructures to replace them (and yet in our residential neighborhoods we allowed huge mansions to be built on small city lots as symbols of the wrong way to go about neighborhood revitalization). Even as the downtown has lost some if its historical purposes—specialty shops and department stores—we are developing a new mixed-use vision for Euclid Avenue. We continue to be frustrated by the sprawling multicounty metropolitan region that divides us by race and class.

Sadly, these years leave us little legacy to build on. But with characteristic resiliency, we move on. In the 1990s the development of the North Coast Harbor area gave Cleveland some international, albeit controversial, architectural notice with I. M. Pei's Rock and Roll Hall of Fame and Museum, Cesar Pelli's Key Office Tower, HOK's Jacobs Field, and the Browns football stadium round out recent downtown development. New midcity housing development is revitalizing some downtown areas with a distinctly suburban twist, and renovated buildings—the Old

This and facing page: Restored interior of Severance Hall, 1931. Walker and Weeks, architects. Restoration 1998–2000, David M. Schwartz Architectural Services. Photograph by Roger Mastrionni.

Arcade, Severance Hall, Huntington Bank, Key Bank, the Sarah Benedict House, and the Cleveland Metropolitan Housing Authority housing—are generating civic pride. The development and renovation of the Playhouse Square Theater complex is of national note and sparkles in an area in need of further development and surrounding amenities.

Various master planning exercises over the past few years—Civic Vision 2000, Cleveland 2010 City Wide Plan, the Lakefront Plan, the Euclid Avenue Corridor, etc.—attempt to give form to our efforts for development and redevelopment. Whether these plans will form a coherent vision that is realistic and appropriate for Cleveland's future remain to be seen. What is distinguished and distinctive for this region seems clear. The vision for the future is ours to develop, and we can practice our regional citizenship on the redevelopments under way. It is one example of the way the quality of our future depends on our ability to think and act. Our challenge is to lift our sites and use everyone's talents—no small dream.

The Artists, Past and Present

What is different about this region is that its strength lies in the artists it has nurtured and who have stayed beyond their learning years to teach and mentor and move about within this area giving it a unique solidarity. Here regionalism is synonymous with the golden age of the Cleveland School in the early part of the century, which was highlighted by experiments in modernism and abstractions from impressionism and realism based on hometown ideals of people, place, industry, labor, and countryside. This resonated with the national American symbolic essence—we *were* America, with our civic leaders dreaming, industry humming, laborers producing, and civility thriving in our cultural and social institutions.

Here it is all about the artists' legacies, influences, relationships. Our cultural heritage was extended through the influence of peers who painted side by side by side—William Sommer, Charles Burchfield, Henry Keller, and William Zorach—and camped out in Ohio's greenlands and discussed and painted what they saw. Abel and Alexander Warshawsky shared ideas from their studies and travels and connected with family, artist friends, and galleries whenever they returned to Cleveland. There is the vitality of the city's industrial strength reflected in the photographs of Margaret Bourke-White and the dialogue between those strong images and the work of Carl Gaertner and others. Cleveland Institute of Art teachers influenced artists such as Marsden Hartley, Roy Lichtenstein, Robert Mangold, Richard Anuszkiewicz, April Gornick, and Joseph Kosuth, who acknowledge the importance of their learning experiences in Cleveland.

While many people, especially since the later decades of the twentieth century, think of New York City as the ideal place for a working artist to live and work, some midcareer artists from Cleveland see the advantages of working right here in this region. In the "Artists, Past and Present" community dialogue, a variety of the area's visual artists participated in a discussion on the importance of place to their artistic sensibilities, and careers.[1]

In addressing the question "How did Cleveland form you as an artist?" painter Michelangelo Lovelace recalled his inner-city childhood and youth:

> I was born and raised in Cleveland. Everything I know—90 percent of my life experience comes out of Cleveland. I grew up in a single-parent household; I grew up in what my friends call "the ghetto" of Cleveland—urban inner city—and went through a lot of the things young people go through growing up in a single-parent household, growing up on the welfare system. So I had a lot of experiences early in my life that formed my opinions and experiences. I dropped out of high school at sixteen. . . . I always drew. It was a way for me to relax, a way for me to get away from the pressures that I had. Once I decided to take my art seriously and once I decided to pursue a career in art . . . Cleveland had the foundation set for me to pursue that goal. . . . Being in Cleveland gave me a richness of life experience, so I grew up fast.

The influence multimedia artist Michael Loderstedt spoke of was how "the impact of the loss of industry has made it possible to work here, own homes, have gardens. . . . Local subject matter gives us a metaphor for the broader view"—and photographer Masumi Hayashi commented that "it is possible to get involved with the community here." Painter/sculptor Don Harvey spoke about the effect the landscape had on him, contrasting it with that of Iowa, where he grew up:

> The landscape in cities like Cleveland intrigues me so much because they are so different from Iowa. It's all about horizons. When I go into the Flats, there's no horizon, the stack is straight up. That might not be so important to me if it hadn't been for the horizon I grew up with.
>
> The landscape of the lake and the Flats immediately became a great influence on me. When I moved here I came straight from graduate school; we were all full of theory and ideas about the future of art and how we were going to affect it. . . . When I came here what I found out about myself is that I am not that kind of artist at all really, that my art comes from the most immediate influence of my surroundings. And it has ever since, so industrial landscapes of Akron and Cleveland eventually evolving into the urban landscape more generally has been my subject matter. They help me realize what kind of artist I am and also have provided me with subject matter and a lot of stimulating experiences.

These expressed influences by the region's current artists provide tremendous insight into their creative processes and further our understanding of the essence of the region's visual arts identity. But it is also important to examine past artists to

see the impact they had on the region. Through exhibits and publications the Cleveland Artists Foundation has examined the work of individual artists and recognized the relationship to and integration with the national and international art movements from the 1920s to 1940s. The tenacity of the Cleveland School's influence on this region's art and its respected place in the American Scene milieu, through a range of naturalistic and modernistic styles, is strong fifty years beyond the bloom.[2]

When we look at the first half of the twentieth century, it is fair to say that without certain key individuals whose enlightened vision and energy galvanized people and opportunity, who nurtured artists and were respected by them, and whose influence and community interests seemed to work together, things might have been quite different. There were those with strong student, teacher, or peer relationships, such as Henry Keller, William Sommer, and Paul Travis; the innovators who created new avenues for artistic expression, examples being Kenneth Bates, Edris Eckhardt, and John Paul Miller; and those whose artistic direction was launched here but whose careers developed elsewhere, including Margaret Bourke-White, Charles Burchfield, and Hughie Lee-Smith. Those included here acknowledged the region's affect upon

Holly Morrison, *Facing North,* 1995–96, gelatin silver print photographs, each 40" x 40". Courtesy of Federal Reserve Bank of Cleveland.

their work, and others listed solidified our sense of who we are with memorable artwork or artwork remembered, such as Elmer Brown and Max Kalish.

In her Preface to the 1993 Cleveland Artist Foundation symposium, *Cleveland as a Regional Art Center*, Karal Ann Marling reminds us that specificity of place can create understanding, sympathy, and respect, that "the art in Cleveland touches our lives in ways too powerful to ignore." Artists who are or were in northeast Ohio created the paintings, ceramics, assemblages, tapestries, and metalwork that reflect who we are. Earlier artists showed us through line and color our land, our people, our work. Present artists challenge us to understand the same as well as the process and to think about such things as the complex results of photographic and printed images. Some reflect on imagery borrowed from history or literature and the metaphors relevant for this time, and others reinvigorate the power of memory, stimulating us to recall images right in front of us that we never see, that we never think about.

The samples of regional artwork have been selected with some major guiding perspectives: distinction, influence, legacy, and accessibility (that the public might be able to see it in the context of exhibits or ongoing). The judgments were made throughout the public discussions by the Creative Essence participants—the public, the speakers, the panelists—or in discussion with May Show organizers, curators, consultants, and gallery directors. Also, the area's art critics and writers of the arts and culture scene played a critical role in framing our views, and mine.

The Visionaries—Gatherers of Peoples and Ideas

William Millikin came to the Cleveland Museum of Art in 1918 as curator of decorative arts and then served as its director from 1930 to 1958, playing a pivotal role in the Cleveland art scene. He was a great director and brought great treasures to Cleveland, buying with discretion and distinction. Not only did Millikin have the generous support of a circle of good and powerful friends, who gave generously of artwork and money to help him build a great museum, but he embraced a community of artists he cared deeply about and had a special commitment to support his "family" of local artists. He did everything possible to nurture the Cleveland contemporary scene, reminding people that all art was contemporary once (something people interested in the art of any "today" are still saying). The May Show, begun in 1919, was his special contemporary treasure.

Another example of his leadership in the arts community was his establishment of Cleveland as a watercolor center, a favorite genre of his. Not only did the May Show include a watercolor category from the start, but he created a number of other special opportunities for the region's watercolorists (including William Sommer, Henry Keller, Paul Travis, Frank Wilcox, and Carl Gaertner). In 1925 the Cleveland Museum of Art (CMA) hosted a large national exhibition, which included twenty-five Cleveland artists whose work had been judged to be of exceptional quality and whose work inspired the judges' comment that, "with proper appreciation and support, there is no reason why Cleveland should not take a foremost place as a watercolor center." In 1934 a similar exhibition, this time international, included forty works by Cleveland artists. He made sure their work was exhibited here and organized traveling exhibitions of watercolor work by contemporary Cleveland artists. In every way he could, Millikin supported local artists.[3]

Clarence Carter, born in Portsmouth, Ohio, attended the Cleveland School of Art and waited tables at the Cleveland Museum of Art. Early on his student paintings caught the attention of William Millikin who became his life-long friend and patron. Carter transformed his observations of life from photographic images into prints and paintings. He drew inspiration from "things close at hand, which are sometimes suffused with memories from the past": funerals and cemeteries, churches and schools, snow scenes, farm scenes, sky and clouds, circus performers. His best-known paintings record specific regional subjects observed in Portsmouth or the industrial centers of the Great Lakes region, making him one of a handful of artists who "paint/speak the language" of northeast Ohio.[4]

Hughie Lee-Smith is arguably the most highly acclaimed African American artist to have started his career in Cleveland. Millikin recognized Lee-Smith's talent early, when he was still only in high school, and saw to it that he got into Saturday classes at the Cleveland Museum of Art. There Henry Keller insisted on "solid drawing, drawing that was alive, vigorous," and Carl Gaertner stressed "the importance of values," often using his night scenes for illustration. He learned lithography while working on the Ohio Youth Project, a government program under the National

Clarence Carter, *William Millikin on His Way to the Century of Progress Exposition*, 1940, oil on canvas 29⅛" x 43⅛". Courtesy of the Cleveland Museum of Art, Mr. and Mrs. William H. Marlatt Fund, courtesy of John and Blake Carter.

Hughie Lee-Smith, *Counterpoise II*, 1989, oil on canvas, 26" x 32". Courtesy of Charles and Frances Debordeau.

Youth Administration that supported his studies at the Cleveland School of Art. His work was "modern" in WPA times and concerned with social realism. He continued to grow as he developed an abstract style that used multiple planes and placed figures in juxtaposition with structures. His work is often mysterious, with unseen faces and backs of women—symbolic, surreal, and classical. His social interests and concerns and personal conflicts are reflected in his work as well as in the isolation and alienation of the artist.[5]

R. Guy Cowan made Cowan Pottery Studios important to American pottery by gathering talent and serving as a mentor throughout the early decades of the twentieth century. The limited editions produced at the Lakewood and Rocky River studios and the freedom granted to the talented young artists working there helped bridge the gap between the handmade pottery of the Arts and Crafts era and the emerging studio pottery movement and also between pottery represented by Rookwood or Weller and others to the art deco and modern designs of Syracuse China, Fiesta Ware, and other potteries that mass produced chinaware.

While 80 percent of the pieces were actually designed by Cowan himself, he did work collaboratively with other artists-designers, including Horace Potter, Thelma Frazier Winter, Waylande Gregory (who was responsible for many production pieces as well as signed limited editions and art deco designs), Russell Aitken, Edris Eckhardt, Herman Matzen, Elmer Novatny, Elsa Vick Shaw, and Frank Wilcox. Viktor Schreckengost worked regularly for Cowan, where he designed his famous Jazz Bowl for Eleanor Roosevelt.

Cowan Pottery's shapes are decorative, graceful, and distinctive, sometimes reminiscent of Oriental ceramics and other times of the luster of English copperware. Glazes are integrated with form. The pottery studio's strengths were not only in the explosion of creative innovation in the work of its artists, but also in the innovative marketing program that incorporated Cowan's belief that his company's designs redefined ceramics as a suitable medium for fine art. Department stores like Halle Brothers and Sterling Welch in Cleveland advertised these modern ceramics in full-page ads, and the company took the products to exhibitions all over the United States.[6]

Horace Potter learned metalsmithing at the Cleveland School of Art and the Boston Society of Arts and Crafts and then honed his craft while studying design and enameling in Europe and from working in Cleveland with such colleague-mentors as Louis Rorimer and R. Guy Cowan. Potter's legacy is in the beautifully crafted display cases and in his unique

Above: Artisans and staff outside the Cowan Pottery display room, spring 1930.

Below: Guy Cowan–Horace Potter, *Mustard Pot,* ca. 1910, earthenware, silver, ivory.

pieces as well as in his counseling of a generation of craftsmen. Silversmith Frederick Miller became Potter's pricipal designer at Potter and Mellen, later becoming an owner. John Paul Miller (no relative) became this area's premier designer and craftsman in gold, rediscovering the ancient art of gold granulation. These two artisans were both mentors to Jim Maszurkewicz, who is Potter and Mellen's Designer-Goldsmith today.[7]

Kalman Kubinyi attended the Cleveland Institute of Art and studied in Munich with his uncle, printmaker Alexander von Kubinyi, before returning to Cleveland to teach printmaking at the John Huntington Polytechnic, the CMA, and the Cleveland School of Art. While he did not abandon oil painting entirely, he spent more and more time making prints—etchings, aquatint, lithography, and "stylotint," which he described as an etching that looks like a lithograph but with a surface with a rich, slightly embossed quality that is stronger than a lithograph yet retains the print's more subtle tones. He is perhaps best known, however, for his leader-

Right: Cowan Pottery Studios, *Flower Frog Figurines,* 1925–31. Courtesy of Rocky River Public Library.

Below left: Horace Potter jewelry designs, early 1940s.

Below right: John Paul Miller, *Cephalopod,* 1978, 18K gold and pure gold with enamel, 3⅛" x 1⅜".

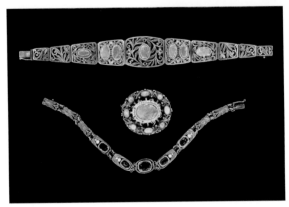

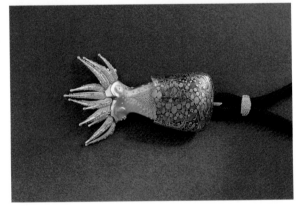

Potter and Mellen display case, ca. 1930s.

ship in the region's printmaking community. Through various organizations he either founded or led, he provided opportunities for member artists—including Henry Keller, William Sommer, Viktor Schreckengost, Edris Eckhardt, and Paul Travis—to work and experiment in the medium of printmaking and to sell their art. However, lively as they were, these efforts, even with support of the directors of both the Cleveland Museum of Art and Cleveland School of Art, were short-lived, as most of these architects, painters, watercolorists, and commercial lithographers diversified their crafts and sought work in other areas.

Between 1935 and 1939 Kubinyi supervised the Graphics Arts Project of the WPA (one of five graphic centers) and then the entire district WPA project. The subjects of many WPA prints were of workers or work scenes with clear social

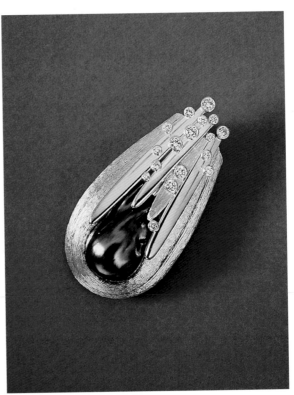

Left: Frederick Miller, pitcher, 1961, sterling silver and ebony, 11½". Courtesy of Smithsonian Institution.

Right: Jim Mazurkewicz, *Comet of the Millenium,* 2000, 18K yellow gold, 1 ct. total weight of diamonds, and Tahitian black pearl, 2" x 1" x ½".

meaning. Angular, sharp, geometric, unsettlingly abstract, even though following the WPA directives to focus on the American scene, Kubinyi's work reflected his sympathy with labor union activities. The idea of his union membership, as well as very liberal leanings, caused anxiety in the arts community.[8]

Henry Keller was arguably the strongest art force in this community during the 1920s and 1930s and is credited with establishing the watercolor tradition in northeast Ohio. First in the area to gain distinction in the medium, Keller used transparent watercolor with tempera and other media and developed techniques that were "widely imitated by his peers" and that used his "extensive knowledge of modern art and aesthetic theory." Equally significant, he was also the region's most respected teacher of watercolor technique. His students include Charles Burchfield, Paul Travis, Frank Wilcox, Carl Gaertner, and Clarence Carter.[9]

Frank Wilcox, a student of Henry Keller's, was a master watercolorist who recreated early Ohio through meticulous research and reporting what he saw in words, drawing, and painting. His paintings, scattered in collections throughout the region, trace Ohio's industrial, agricultural and economic growth, lifting the art of watercolor in their wonderful "directness and economy of means." In addition to Keller, Wilcox's mentors include Frederick Gottwald and Louis Rorimer, whom he joined, in 1913, on the faculty of the Cleveland School of Art, where he taught drawing, painting, design, and printmaking for forty years and mentored students like Charles Burchfield and Carl Gaertner.[10]

Charles Burchfield, a master watercolorist, honed his artistic skills at the Cleveland School of Art with mentor-teachers Frederick Gottwald, Henry Keller, and Frank Wilcox. Several of his teachers, including Henry Keller, encouraged him to be an independent artist even though his talents in design were clear. During the 1915–16 period, his examination of the effects of light, atmosphere, weather, time of day, and seasons replaces the more posterlike decorative art he was doing as

Kalman Kubinyi, *Railroad Crossing,* ca. 1935–39, lithograph, 14" x 9¾". Courtesy of Special Collections, Case Western Reserve University.

Henry Keller, *View of Cleveland,* ca. 1930, watercolor on paper, 18¾" x 12¾". Courtesy of Cleveland Artists Foundation, gift of Dorothy Beck.

part of his studies. In 1921 he moved to Buffalo, where he worked as a wallpaper designer until 1929, when he became a full-time painter. He never forgot his Ohio and Cleveland roots; throughout his career the region's landscapes—the neighborhoods, parks, suburbs, waterways, and countryside—inspired his work.[11]

William Sommer, primarily a watercolorist, was a valuable and beloved member to the arts community in Cleveland in the early decades of the twentieth cen-

tury. Sommer was also active among the artists here as a leader of the Kokoon
Arts Club (1911–46) whose members, among them August Biehle, Henry Keller,
and Hart Crane, met often to draw and paint, exhibit, and celebrate. While friend
and supporter Hart Crane tried to lure Sommer to New York, where he would
meet people who could help him become better appreciated as an artist, Sommer
opted to stay here, where, from his summer retreat at Brandywine, he could paint
the hills, valleys, grazing cattle, old frame farmhouses, and people in his own
modern vein. Breaking from the small watercolor format, he painted the mural
The City in 1833 in the Brett Hall of the Cleveland Public Library, which follows
WPA directives for American scene subjects.[12]

Artists Who Invented

Margaret Bourke-White moved to Cleveland in 1927 ready to pursue a career in
landscape and architectural photography. Commissioned to photograph, for pro-
motional purposes, the suburban estates of Cleveland's corporate leaders, White
earned enough to allow her to be able to spend her free time developing her evocative explorations of the modern machine and factory. In a short intense two years
here she developed a cadre of clients from the city's leading industrialists and their
corporations and a full portfolio of photographs of the industrial Flats. Her photographs of the Flats, the working steel mills, the Terminal Tower, the smokestacks,
and tugboats and ore boats showed her to be a romantic artist in a mechanical

August Biehle, Kokoon Club poster, 1937, lithograph, 21" x 13". Courtesy of Joseph and Elaine Kisvardai.

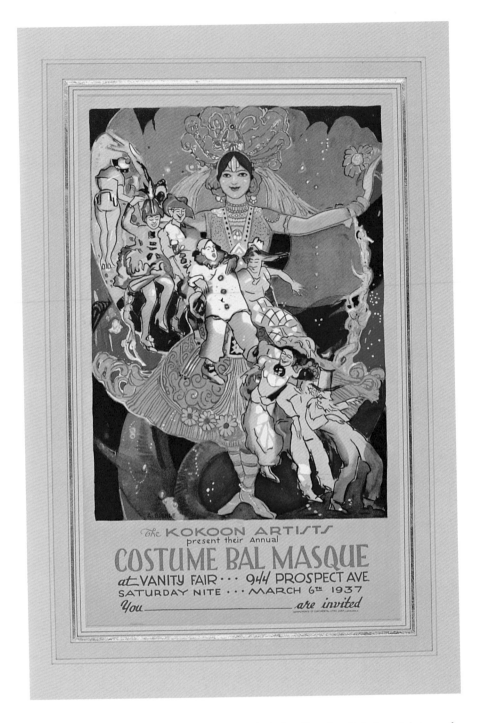

and industrial milieu as she established symbols for Cleveland's industrial strength. She was so successful that by 1929 she was off to New York to do a photo essay assignment for Henry Luce's new magazine, *Fortune*. Cleveland had served as a staging ground for successful connections with national media and wide opportunities for the rest of her career.[13]

Kenneth Bates always wanted to be an artist and a teacher. The dean of American enamelists, who also taught and influenced many generations of American students as one of first in the field in this country, he imbued this art form with his horticulturalist sensitivities and his innate sense of design. While many of his pieces are based on purely abstract designs, most patterns can be traced to the natural world, with many shapes and ideas gleaned from his lakeside home.

Edris Eckhardt is known nationally and internationally for her work in both ceramics and glass and is credited with rediscovering the Egyptian art of fusing gold leaf between sheets of glass to produce gold glass, a technique that had eluded artists for 2,000 years. She developed her glassmaking to include bronze and glass

Margaret Bourke-White, *Blast Furnace Operator with "Mud Gun" Otis Steel Company,* ca. 1928, gelatin silver print, 13" x 10¼". Courtesy of Cleveland Museum of Art, gift of Mrs. Albert A. Levin. Reprinted with permission of the Estate of Margaret Bourke-White.

Kenneth Bates, *Oriental Casket*, 1966, cloisonné, 2" x 1½" x 3". Courtesy of Joseph and Elaine Kisvardai. Photograph by Bernie Rich.

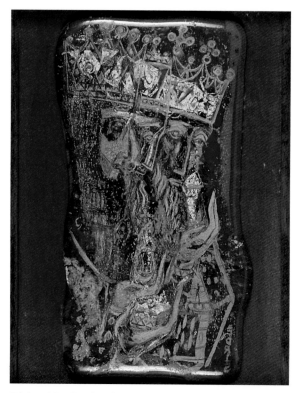

Edris Eckhardt, *The Three Ages of Man*, 1956, gold glass, 7¼" x 4". Courtesy of Elaine and Joseph Kisvardi. Photograph by Bernie Rich.

combinations, which some think her best accomplishment. Her subjects ranged from those out of storybooks (as with her 1937 Alice in Wonderland series exhibited at the World's Fair in Paris) to the complex theme of the illustrated piece. She taught ceramics at the Cleveland School of Art and was this region's supervisor for sculpture for the Federal Arts Project. She opened minds so that later glass artists in the region, like Brent Kee Young and Henry Halem, could carry the art of glassmaking to further experimentation and invention.[14]

Public Icons in Cleveland's History

Elmer Brown, who had served time in a Missouri state prison chain gang for illegally riding freight trains, came to Cleveland in 1929. He was one of a group of talented African American artists who were influenced in some way by Karamu, the Cleveland Playhouse Settlement established by Rowena and Russell Jelliffe in 1915. Through Karamu, he and artists Charles Sallee, Hughie Lee-Smith, and several others were given opportunities and contacts that allowed their talent to grow and flourish, and they were able to train under mentors like Paul Travis, Henry Keller, Viktor Schreckengost, Carl Gaertner, and Edris Ekhardt and come in contact with poet Langston Hughes, dancer Katherine Dunham, writer Zora Neal Hurston, among many major talents in the arts. "These rich experiences, which were unique to Cleveland, Ohio in the 1930s and 1940s, enabled these artists to develop a character of sophistication unrivaled by any of their African-American contemporaries working elsewhere in America."[15] Perhaps because of the influence of Karamu, the CMA, John Huntington Polytechnic Institute, and the Cleveland School of Art opened their doors to African Americans.

Brown was an active WPA artist, producing murals, linoleum prints, portrait paintings, and ceramic sculpture. He painted his *Free Speech* mural, in Cleveland's City Club, in 1942 when he was employed by

Charles Louis Sallee Jr., *Anna,* ca. 1936, oil on canvas, 43" x 33". Courtesy of Dr. Albert C. Antoine and Mrs. June Sallee Antoine.

the Works Progress Administration. One of the most important murals in the city, it represents the City Club's respect for justice, freedom, honor, and the free exchange of ideas.

Max Kalish, a prominent sculptor, was selected to design and build the statue of Abraham Lincoln that stands outside the Cleveland Board of Education building. Kalish's talent was recognized at the Cleveland School of Art and by mentors with whom he worked in New York and Paris. He was in dialogue with other artists of his time and noted for his sculptures of laborers. A well-honed community tale, the Lincoln statue was the idea of the *Cleveland Press,* which in 1923 had initiated a drive to raise money for its construction, and in one short week Cleveland schoolchildren raised $30,000 in pennies and nickels. It may be the only work of Kalish's displayed out of doors.[16]

Teachers, Teaching, and Legacy

Paul Travis learned from his teacher Henry Keller, who is remembered for his belief in the importance of observation and drawing. After his stint in World War I in France, where he enlarged his tour of duty to include the opportunity to sketch and paint what he saw, Travis returned home to begin his teaching career at the Cleveland School of Art, where he became one of the region's most beloved teachers for almost forty years. Travis's trip to Africa in 1927–28, sponsored by several institutions, produced sensitive paintings of the people and energetic paintings of the animals. The recent "discovery" of *Masai Lionhunt,* a major work by Travis that has not been seen in Cleveland since he received first prize for it in the 1928 May Show, is the story of many regional artworks. This painting, a definitive statement about Africa, had been acquired by Russell Aitkin, a noted ceramic artist, international socialite, and big-game hunter who had studied with Travis and knew his work, and recently turned up in one of his estate sales at Christies.[17]

Carl Gaertner was born and raised in the Great Lakes region and understood it well, and anyone who encounters his work in the Cleveland Museum of Art, Huntington Bank, Baldwin-Wallace College, or the many homes of admirers and collectors can see its power. A testament to his teaching and his place in the American regionalist movement, Hughie Lee-Smith said that Gaertner "teaches all of us the power and alienation of the growing industrial city—the dark brooding images of

Paul Travis, *The Syndics,* 1946, oil on masonite, 31½" x 50", depicting Cleveland School of Art faculty, including Kenneth Bates, Frank Wilcox, Willard Combes, Otto Edge, Glen Sherwood, and Rolf Stoll. Courtesy of Cleveland Artists Foundation, gift of Elisabeth and Michael Dreyfuss.

Above: Carl Gaertner, *Bend on the Storm King*, gouache and oil, 24"x 39". Courtesy of Frances and Seth Taft. Photograph by Rob Muller.

Left: Carl Gaertner, *Steel Mills on the Cuyahoga*, 1928, oil on canvas, 24½" x 28¾". Courtesy of Hahn Loeser & Parks LLP.

industry, especially the massive structures of the steel industry lying in the midst of soot and grime and under the heavy clouds that Clevelanders knew well." Peopled with the blue-collar workers, his paintings were metaphors for the troubling time of the Depression, and as with Bourke-White, these industrial subjects became elegant in Gaertner's hands. While beginning in the 1920s Gaertner's industrial subject paintings won many first prizes in the May Show, he, like Wilcox, Keller, Travis, Biehle, Deike, and Sommer, also painted nature and the countryside. Among his regular excursions away were those along the Hudson River, where he would sketch the scenery.[18]

Viktor Schreckengost, by temperament and talent, is always solving design problems, always thinking creatively, and is always exciting to his students and so represents the epitome of the best aspects of the Cleveland art scene. His career has been so varied that we could easily be captivated by his sculptures, ceramics, or paintings, but it is his leadership in the industrial design area that is his legacy. First and foremost a creative thinker and inspiring teacher, it was clearly these qualities that have endeared him to peers, students, clients, and friends over more than fifty years developing and chairing the Industrial Design Department at the Cleveland Institute of Art. The challenges of problem solving for corporate clients were handled so deftly that his innovations became standards, especially in ceramics and toy design. Scrap metal in the automobile industry became the raw material for pedal cars or tricycles; dripping glazes at Cowan Pottery became new colors or techniques. He was an inspiration because he was always inventing. And it is likely that, because of his role in early modern bicycle design and his ties to Murray Ohio, Huffy, and the Sears catalog, that every one of us over fifty has owned a bicycle influenced by the design skills of Viktor Schreckengost.[19]

Viktor Schreckengost among his pedal cars, 1959, which were created from scraps of metal from automobile manufacturers.

Nottingham-Spirk Design Associates, Little Tikes Kitchen, 1977–90, rotational molded plastic, 17" x 15" x 36".

John Nottingham and *John Spirk* are among the most successful of Schreckengost's student-disciples. After graduating from the Cleveland Institute of Art in 1972, they founded Nottingham-Spirk Design Associates, one of the leading new-product design invention and development groups in the country. Among their major clients is Little Tikes, for whom they designed more than 250 of their safe and winning toys.

William McVey, sculptor and teacher, inspired his students with his wisdom about the potential of sculpture and the striving toward accessibility—"the presentation of the sculptural idea in a form acceptable and meaningful to the intelligent layman, without sacrificing quality." McVey's work can be found across the country, with forty-eight pieces of his public sculpture in northeast Ohio, including the grizzly bear at the Cleveland Museum of Natural History, a bust of Hart Crane, and his last work, the *Tom Johnson Monument*, in the courtyard of the Western Reserve Historical Society.[20]

John Clague studied painting and sculpture at the Cleveland Institute of Art, at a time when many of the "masters" of the Cleveland School—Kenneth Bates, Frank Wilcox, Viktor Schreckengost, Edris Eckhardt, Paul Travis—were still teaching and early in the careers of the region's new, influential artists, among them William McVey. Before beginning his own teaching career—first at Oberlin College and then at the Cleveland Institute of Art—he studied and traveled on prestigious fellowships. His work in both painting and sculpture range from the figurative to the abstract, and through a multitude of approaches in between. He credits this with enabling him to "enter the world of each of my students prepared to deal with their unique range of sensibilities allowing me to reinforce their approach and hopefully provide the tools they needed to achieve their full potential."

Clague's work itself embraces a range of sensibilities. Some are bold abstract forms in bronze, steel, or fiberglass with black-and-white or multicolored surfaces. Some are kinetic sculptures that move or make sounds. Some are small, highly polished stainless steel reliefs. And some stand tall, like the 1960 bronze *Flower of Erebus* that greeted Cleveland Museum of Art visitors at the front door of the lobby for years.[21]

Joseph McCullough returned to Cleveland in 1952 to teach at his alma mater, the Cleveland Institute of Art, bringing with him the exciting ideas of Joseph Albers, world-famous artist and color theorist at Yale University. He integrated Albers's experiments and demonstrations in the study and teaching of color theory—illustrating reversed grounds, space, and vibrating boundaries and the "many faces of color"—into his own popular and influential color theory course, "Color and Light." McCullough's own favorite painting is *Red Sound,* inspired by the sounds and images of nature, deemed bold, expressive, and stunning. Sherman Lee, former director of the Cleveland Museum of Art, said of McCullough's work: "If one understands that the ultimate use of color . . . is in the sensory messages perceived, recognized and then related to a general theory or vision of nature, then one can understand the images made by those artists who are fully alive before nature."[22]

Edwin Mieczkowski attended the Cleveland Institute of Art in the 1950s as a student and then spent the next four and a half decades creating vital art and teaching at the Cleveland Institute of Art and informally in his "Idea Garage," a place for discussion about the arts and philosophy. Just as the Institute gave him a firm foundation for his painting, his influence on friends, students, and peers over the years has been enormous. His career was launched when he, Julian Stanzcak, Frank Hewitt, and Richard Anuszkiewicz of the Cleveland Institute of Art participated in the "Responsive Eye" show at the Museum of Modern Art in 1965.[23]

Mieczkowski's works have long been based in neo-constructivism, the anti–abstract expressionist movement that embraced geometric forms. His current work turns away from geometric forms and reflects his newer intense bionic phase. Large, energetic, imposing, the paintings consume the viewer with their energy and vitality. One can only be impressed by his excitement and effervescence.

Printmaking

Cleveland's artists who worked with Maurico Lasansky, who taught printmaking at the University of Iowa from 1945 to 1984, were connected with the evolution of printmaking in this country. H. C. Cassill, Jean Kubota Cassill, David Haberman, Gerald Kramea, and Phyllis Seltzer were among them. Lasansky still creates new prints today, but the peak of his influence was in the 1950s. Mention of his contributions can be found in every book on the subject. He stressed experimentation, pushed back the technical boundaries of printmaking, enlarged the scale of prints, and achieved nuances and luminosity in his colors through the use of multiple plates. He felt that unlike a scientific discovery, which is soon surpassed by another, a true work of art is timeless.

Printmaking is an honored art form. Visiting collections of prints—works on paper—in museums, libraries, and private homes is especially gratifying. People interested in collecting, especially modern art, often invest in graphic arts because the work is more affordable. And almost every artist has made prints at some time during his or her career. In today's art world, given the many ways of making prints, that is even truer. Prints and photographs are basic to many multimedia works, so it is rarer to find the artist who seeks a printmaking career.[24]

In the 1978 exhibition "The Printmakers Work," sponsored by NOVA, the work of twenty regional printmakers spanned almost fifty years. This exhibit linked the traditional and experimental work of the artists who produced them as fine, not commercial, art. The exhibition lined up the time-honored methods—intaglio processes, woodcuts, monoprints, linocuts, etchings—side by side with the newer serigraphs, ozalid print, relief molds, xerography, or complex and multiple methods in color or black and white. They reflected American scene subjects, serial images, and social messages in abstract and naturalistic styles. And while the prints of the earlier years could be measured in inches, many done after the 1950s could be measured in feet.

H. C. Cassill came to Cleveland from Iowa in 1957 to head the Printmaking Department at the Cleveland Institute of Art. He expanded what had been a small department to one in which a student could major at the time the Institute was gearing up for full accreditation. Even if they weren't headed for a career as printmakers, students were heard to say, "If you don't do anything else, take Cassill." For more than 30 years, he inspired generations of students. Cassill can be credited with changing the way this region saw printmaking as his talents and those he

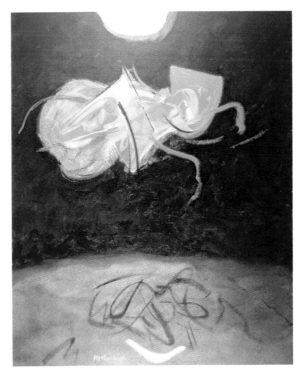

Joseph McCullough, *Red Sounds,* 1967, acrylic, 40" x 50". Courtesy of Betty and Osman K. Mawardi.

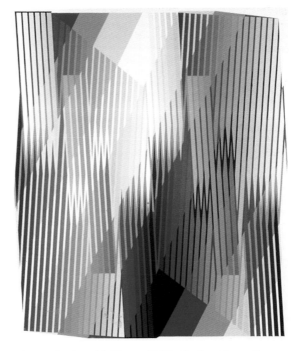

Edwin Mieczkowski, *Blue and White Ford,* 1966, acrylic on canvas, 47" x 41.5". Courtesy of Cleveland Museum of Art, Wishing Well Fund.

H. C. Cassill, *Icarus*, 1958,
intaglio, 27¾" x 20½".

influenced infiltrated the May Show and galleries. His intaglio prints, which demand great care and accuracy in their preparation, have always been multilayered in content and context. His work is at once reflective, philosophical, evocative, and intense.

Phyllis Sloane is equally well recognized for her painting and printmaking. Honored as a printmaker who explored many different techniques—wood, linoleum, and cork cuts, lithography and silkscreen; transfer prints and color etchings—she created magnificently designed and crafted work. As a painter she creates similar thematic series, portraits, and still lifes with the same perfect precision

of placement, balancing negative and positive space and color to stunning results. Sloane was as prolific as she was talented, and her work is in many homes and public places throughout the region.[25]

Phyllis Seltzer has always been interested in the process of printmaking. She uses a heat transfer method to produce work that is of vibrant color. Since 1986 Seltzer has made tremendous advances in technologies of electrostatic-copier/heat transfer prints. These prints begin with an oil painting made from sketches and photographs; Seltzer then divides the completed painting into sizes compatible with the imagery and the size of the new paper. After the prints are trimmed and glued together, they are placed in a press to create a final heat-transfer print on paper. This paper is coated with a special emulsion that absorbs and holds the colors via an electrically charged field. This process allows Seltzer to create prints on a scale larger than permitted by conventional graphic media. She derives inspiration from her immediate environment but uses innovative printmaking techniques to translate these experiences into indelibly personal images. She has been a leader in the art community, contributing to groups such as EAT (Experiments in Art and Technology) and has established a national reputation for her creative application of new technologies in the graphic arts, including research in color xerography, pochoir ozalid, and heat transfer prints.[26]

Left: Phyllis Sloane, *Still Life with Still Life Drawings*, 1987, acrylic on canvas, 48" x 54".

Right: Phyllis Sloane, *Paul Travis*, 1970, serigraph, 29¼" x 25½". Courtesy of Cleveland Artists Foundation, gift of the artist.

The Art of Crafts — Clay, Textile, Glass

The crafts departments at the Cleveland Institute of Art have been led since the 1950s by talented artists who are key figures in their disciplines. Edris Eckhardt's, Kenneth Bates's, and John Paul Miller's discoveries and uses of old or ancient techniques and Toshiko Takaezu's work in bringing sensitivity to new forms helped break down the barriers between crafts and fine arts. By the 1960s there was an

Phyllis Seltzer, *Dichotomy (L)*, 2000, Ed 10, heat-transfer print, 50" x 38", State of Ohio Office Building, Columbus.

exchange of ideas across disciplines and cultures as artists explored concepts in more than one art form. Weavers became ceramists, and potters tried sculptors' processes.

Toshiko Takaezu came to the Cleveland Institute of Art in 1955 to expand its ceramics program. Chair for ten years, she transformed our thinking about what it means to work with clay and in doing so set the stage for the future, inspiring peers and students, such as Claude Conover. Blending her Japanese heritage with a Western aesthetic, her pots are simple in design, natural and eloquent. Her "closed form," for which she is well known, is sculptural rather than like standard vessels or containers. Many times asymmetrical, they are deeply colored and totally unique. In the second half of the twentieth century, Toshiko Takaezu has helped transform ceramics into a major medium of artistic expression in America and forged her place as a master ceramist in the American craft movement. She left Cleveland to join the faculty at Princeton University, where she remained for the next twenty-five years until retiring in 1992. Her clay remains alive and responsive to her command as she continues to make art every day.[27]

Judith Salomon designs for form over function and is inspired by architectural form. Her artwork explores the whole meaning and use of a piece, how insides and outsides work together—the idea of "containers and containment." Fun to look at and use, her colorful, playful, imaginative, and sculptural vessels, plates, bowls, and tea and sake sets are especially inviting. They have a distinct look as she experiments with color, lines, planes, contrast, design, matte, and high-gloss glazes. Salomon joined the faculty at the Cleveland Institute of Art in 1977 and has enjoyed a rich teaching life with students, guiding them through the creative process and nurturing their development as artists.[28]

Kirk Mangus, a ceramicist and sculptor who teaches at Kent State University, works in a completely different way. His vessels "borrow the sensibility of early Asian ceramics and volume from the classic Greek vases," and the carvings are multilayered and contemporary, giving them an irreverent and insolent feel. He often uses a wood-fired kiln and controls the effects by monitoring the length of firing and the arrangement within the kiln.[29]

Toshiko Takaezu, *Star Series,* 1999–2000, 11 pieces, glazed stoneware, to 67" x 28" x 28" diameter. Courtesy of Racine Art Museum, gift of the artist.

Above left: Claude Conover, *Chab*, 1961, stoneware, 19" x 16". Courtesy of Elaine and Joseph Kisvardai.

Above right: Judith Salomon, *Platter* (part of a series), 2001, white earthenware clay, 23" round x 3½" depth. Courtesy of University Hospitals Chagrin Headlands Medical Center.

Right: Kirk Mangus, *Big Bug Jar*, 1989, wood-fired stoneware, 29" x 15" diameter. Courtesy of British Petroleum.

Traditional and Innovative Textiles

The textile arts, called weaving or fiber arts, have taken many new directions in the last three decades. The works represented in exhibits of the Textile Arts Alliance (organized as the Textile Arts Club in 1934, with its first exhibit in 1936) at the Cleveland Museum of Art and Beck Center have pointed to the varieties of style (tight, loose, knotted, sculptural, appliquéd), material (wool, silk, synthetic fibers), texture (smooth, bumpy, regular, irregular), and subject (traditional, representation, social).

Leza McVey started out her artistic career as a ceramist, but a deteriorating eye condition led her to textile design and production. She became known for creating original designs using traditional weaving methods.

Lilian Tyrrell uses the technical brilliance of her large-scale tapestries to confront the viewer with some of society's pressing and provocative issues. Traditionally, tapestry weaves social, religious, and philosophic issues into the tableaux; Tyrrell expresses contemporary problems and conditions. Her images are from the realm of global issues and social values. Her abstract forms are beautiful, her woven images powerful, her colors strong.[30]

Glass

Glass has become important in the last fifty years. Jay Hoffman, who wrote *A Study in Regional Taste*, a retrospective of the May Shows from 1919 to 1975, rightly credits the development of the medium to schools and universities that provide the resources necessary for blowing and casting—the large and expensive kilns

Leza McVey, *Detail of Rug*, colored squares of woolen material, 9' x 9'. Courtesy of Frances and Seth Taft. Photograph by Rob Muller.

and specialized equipment. The explanation for the high degree of interest in glass in this region is stimulated by the fact that the studio glass movement in America started in 1962 with significant glassblowing workshops jointly led by Dominick Labino, a Johns Mansville fiber glass artist, and Henry Littleton, a ceramist sponsored by the Toledo Art Museum.[31]

Brent Kee Young, on the Cleveland Institute of Art faculty, is perhaps best known for glass of simple cylindrical forms with inclusions that suggest fossilized animals. His work transforms glass into objects of art using abstract ideas and mostly recognizable forms. Not unlike the Tyrrell tapestry, Young fuses traditional craft (glassmaking) with contemporary form.

Henry Halem wrote *Glass Notes* (1996), a seminal text for students of glassmaking, as a reminder of his own ideals and as inspiration for others to stay involved and find the satisfaction that making art and glass can bring. He is noted especially for his experimentation with flat glass that resulted in an exposition of painting with hot glass; he frames the images, which are two- and three-dimensional, and uses a painter's technique to create abstract designs on it. He has also created work that assembles images in a collage technique. He taught glassmaking at Kent State University for twenty-nine years.

Left: Brent Kee Young, *Fossil Series.* "*Worlds . . . Apart,*" 1993, blown glass and 23K gold leaf, carved bass wood base, ca. 15" x 10".

Right: Henry Halem, *Roman Display Vessel,* 2001, glass and aluminum, 21" x 17" x 6".

Photography

Douglas Lucak is a Cleveland native whose work focuses on the urban and industrial communities of northeast Ohio. His stated goal is "to convey more about the human condition than literal depiction of the urban landscape." Although he began working with a panoramic camera, he has since relied on pinhole cameras he fashions himself. The small prints he creates evoke haunting feelings of abandonment and danger, often associated with the decaying urban environment. He frequently enhances the inherent moody and atmospheric qualities of his images by adding shades of toner.[32]

Penny Rakoff has an astute understanding of color and light, and this is evident in her images. Trained in painting at the University of Michigan, Rakoff translated her interest in color theory and composition to her photographic work. By controlling and manipulating natural and artificial light in extended nighttime exposures, she conjures spectral, often surreal displays from otherwise banal subject matter. Her interest has evolved into public art, site-specific installations, and community.[33]

Masumi Hayashi uses her photographic collages, made from images of a variety of subjects—landscapes and interiors, beautiful and ugly—to speak to memory and recollection. As one critic has said of her work, "While the form of the original is apparent, it has been changed by the hand of the artist, just as memories are altered by the peculiarities of our psyches." Her best-known work is "American Concentration Camps," which captures the desolate, isolated areas of the West where Japanese Americans, like her and her family, were interred during World War II.[34]

Christopher Pekoc, though he studied painting and drawing at Kent State University, considers himself to be self-taught. He began by using photographs to aid him with his portraits and landscape drawings and then used collage as a starting point in his paintings; these collaged studies in turn became airbrush paintings in

Douglas Lucak, *Radiance and Industry,* 1995, black-and-white photograph, oil paint, 2¾" x 7⅛".

Penny Rakoff, *Nightscape on the Cuyahoga #1*, 1987, Ekta-color print, 14¾" x 18⅞". Courtesy of Akron Art Museum, purchased with funds donated by Beatrice K. McDowell.

Below: Masumi Hayashi, *Public Square, Cleveland, Ohio*, 1994, panoramic photo collage, 20" x 56".

the 1970s and, in the 1980s, large pastels. Interaction with human presence stimulates his creative effort much differently than the clippings of inanimate objects from magazines. The specific choices he makes about the images relies on his sense of aesthetic balance and intuitive symbolism, which results in a complex message for the viewer. The process includes shellacking the surface before assembling the pieces that achieves an overall effect of a beautiful old manuscript. The message of the additionally scratched surface may be ominous and evocative. Just like human life itself—imperfect and fragmented– and scarred.[35]

Sculpture

Because sculpture is a three-dimensional artwork that is most often accessible to the public, it may well be one of the most important and lasting of the contemporary visual arts. Pre-1940s public sculpture at street intersections, in public squares or public parks, usually in bronze or marble, commemorate people or events, and interior sculpture pieces, usually pedestal statuary placed in museums and galleries, likely feature figures or portrait busts. After World War II sculptors began creating artworks in a wide variety of abstract shapes, weights, sizes, surfaces, and materials.

David Davis was "turned on" to sculpture in John Clague's Wednesday-evening class at the Cleveland Institute of Art in the late 1960s. He confided to Clague his plan to break with American Greetings, where he was a vice president of the Creative Department, and devote his life to sculpture. Setting up a metalworking studio in a former gasoline station in Cleveland Heights, he started to pursue his Harmonic Grid sculptures, mostly in metal, based on a restricted vocabulary of triangles, circles, and rectangles that he divided and combined into systems of logical structures. In the 1980s he started exploring the tetrahedron, arch, and spiral, whose softened edges lent themselves to wood and stone.

He spent nearly forty years creating a large, impressive sculptural oeuvre distinguished by its pervasive quality, variety, visual intelligence, and originality. The consistency of his sculpture achievement is attributable partly to his unflinching adherence to certain philosophical principles, such as respecting materials, exercising intellectual control over the creative process, and developing extensive permutations of a visual idea over a long period of time. He pursued some motifs for more than a decade, as reflected in the eight major themes of his sculpture: Open Forms, Growth Bands, Walking, Harmonic Grids, Tetrahedrons, Arches, Gates, and Sound Towers. He made significant contributions to the vitality of the sculpture profession in this region both in terms of his own sculptures and the institutions he created: the Sculpture Center and the Artists Archives of the Western Reserve.[36]

Gene Kangas earned a Master of Fine Arts degree in sculpture and taught art at the university level for thirty-two years at Cleveland State University. He gained

Christopher Pekoc, *Ritual of Inquiry,* 1998, mixed media on electrostatic prints, paper, and polyester film with machine stitching, 26½" x 103". Courtesy of Case Western Reserve University, Baer and Hiltner Collection.

Left: David Davis, *David Berger National Memorial Monument*, 1974, corten steel, 14' x 11' x 11'. Courtesy of Mayfield Jewish Community Center, Cleveland Heights, Ohio.

Right above: Gene Kangas, *Hart Crane Memorial*, 1995, painted steel and corten. Courtesy of Ohio Canal Corridor.

Right below: Athena Tacha, *Tension Arches*, 1975, painted stainless steel, 12' x 24' x 2'.

public recognition as an artist via commissions to design, build, and install large site-specific sculptures, such as those at the State Office building, at the Justice Center, and on the Case Western Reserve campus. A significant example of his work is his memorial to poet Hart Crane. Today Kangas's focus has evolved into narratives in wood using a state-of-the-art lathe. Sculptures, which once portrayed figural steel profiles, have evolved into portraits cut in reverse.[37]

Athena Tacha is recognized nationally as a pioneer in the field of site sculpture. Her public career began with a piece commissioned by the Cleveland Area Arts Council for the 1976 celebration of the nation's Bicentennial. Her first site-specific piece designed for a particular location, now located in front of the Music and Communications Building at Cleveland State University, *Tension Arches* invites pedestrians to experience its triangular openings and twelve-foot-high ogee arches. Painted red on one side and green on the other, the color shifts as you move by it, and the tones and shadows change with the time of day. Tacha was professor of sculpture at Oberlin College from 1973 until 1998.[38]

Brinsley Tyrrell, an emeritus professor of art at Kent State University, was known to be a very charismatic and generous teacher. Tyrrell retired to focus full time on his many outside commissions, among them those that appear on the Kent State University and Case Western Reserve University campuses and, most recently, the

Brinsley Tyrrell, *Salt of the City,* 1996 and 2000, salt sculpture.

fifty-nine iron fences circling tree islands embellishing the commercial area of Coventry Road in Cleveland Heights.

While serving on the artistic design team for Cleveland's new Waterfront Line, Tyrrell took a tour of the salt mines under Lake Erie. He became fascinated by the extensive salt deposits that lie beneath Cleveland and Lake Erie and began to explore the different properties of salt. He carved an architectural sculpture series from salt blocks, sandstone, and other materials from the region. The salt statute was designed for outdoor installation so that it would evolve as rain and the elements reshape it (indeed, after eight years it is disappearing into the sidewalk). Combining the salt blocks with steel, concrete, and sandstone, Tyrrell tried to capture Cleveland's urban feel: "These are basic materials that have a strong association with Cleveland. You find most of these materials in the city's buildings."[39]

Johnny Coleman teaches African American studies and sculpture/interdisciplinary media at Oberlin College. The raw and found materials incorporated in *Northern Ohio Crossroads* tell a lot about Johnny Coleman's concerns and body of work. In this piece he sought to unearth the stories of the African Americans who came north during the Great Migration and inhabited the city's neighborhoods. Integral to the

Johnny Coleman, *Northern Ohio Crossroads,* 1996, various metals and man-made materials, "Urban Evidence: Contemporary Artists Reveal Cleveland," SPACES.

work are interviews he conducted with several generations of black Clevelanders, and the materials include rusted tin gathered from fallen roofs lining the walls, collard greens growing in clay pots set in an oversized wheelbarrow, dried flowers gathered from vacant lots, found wooden doors and windows, treated tar paper, found silk ties—the "stuff" of the city and its people.[40]

Painting

In the last decades most Ohio painters can be called "regional" only because they live here. They are most usually identified with their places of teaching or their gallery exhibitions. With few exceptions, there are no unifying stylistic tendencies. Styles are short-lived; the pluralistic "scene" changes fast. And greater mobility and accessibility afforded by easy travel and communication have almost eliminated geographical boundaries.

However, William Robinson, curator of Modern and European Art at the Cleveland Museum of Art, after reviewing an exhibit that compared, side by side, twenty East Village/Soho artists with twenty Ohio artists, noted that "in contrast to the self-indulgent and superficiality of the East Village art, the Ohio art seemed to reflect a more serious attitude and sense of purpose." He attributed this to the fact that many of the Ohio artists are professional teachers not as driven to compete for sales and attention in the New York media. The works here are distinguished by their originality, seriousness of purpose, and powerful feeling.[41]

Julian Stanczak, a displaced Pole, migrated to the United States after World War II and enrolled in the Cleveland Institute of Art. It was his close examination of Paul Klee's sense of color and his ability to "make memories abstract," as well as his work with Joseph Albers, the color theorist at Yale after he graduated from CIA, that empowered him to pursue self-expression through color and abstract form. Always interested in the movements of the cosmos, and how it remakes itself in vast and infinitesimal ways, he was eager to project the way in which color and line interact. He wanted to shape himself into a translating device for ambient impressions, something best achieved later when he could use acrylic paints and tape for making perfect lines. His work was noticed early, and he exhibited in Ohio and New York, where he won prizes and his perceptual art was deemed "impressive and important."[42]

John Pearson first came to Cleveland as the International Artist in Residence at the Cleveland Institute of Art, 1970–72; for the next thirty years he was professor of art at Oberlin College. In his early work he examined "art as system"—work carefully organized around sequences of shapes, colors, lines, beginning with an idea that has multiple possibilities for satisfying resolutions. He selected color schemes and programmed small motifs within isometric grids according to self-invented formulas in order to achieve a satisfying aesthetic result. He devised an

Julian Stanczak, *City Mural*, 1973, 12-story fresco on the Carter Manor building.

arithmetic scheme to realize an idea and then preplanned a process that determined the beginning, middle, and end of the work, expunging all romanticism in the way he applied color. Within a set of parameters, he examined all possibilities of positioning modules to examine how color looked in different circumstances in his orderly arrangement of elements.

John Pearson, *Mondrian Linear Series*, 1977, silk-screen inks on acrylic over canvas, 210" x 660" x 4", Cleveland Justice Center.

Douglas Max Utter, *The World Long Ago*, 1991, mixed paint media on canvas, 66" x 50".

Ken Nevadomi, *Man Who Lived in a Refrigerator*, 1985, acrylic, 66" x 66".

By not working out of social or political issues, or natural or man-made forms, Pearson uses color and form to capture deeper spiritual intangibles, timeless universals such as breath, heartbeat, and heavens, to probe to the innermost core. Pearson's work has evolved into related but profoundly different expressions over time; his has been an evolution beyond strict geometry (especially the grid) to harmonic forms abstracted from nature.[43]

Douglas Max Utter continues the traditions of Western depiction in his figurative canvases—but with a change in focus. Over the past two decades the subjects of his works have been either iconographic or deeply personal. In general they explore the overlap between the metaphors of religion and poetic art, the conventions of realistic paintings, and the experience of his own family life. Often working with unconventional paint media, like latex house paint, spray paint, or various asphalt commercial substances, his portraits of family members and close friends often refer to Christian or neo-classical concerns. For him these contextual shifts are a jumping-off point for painterly meditations about the integration of tactile and psychological experience in terms of the realities of the contemporary world. Also a writer, he is senior editor of *Angle*, a nonprofit journal of arts and culture.[44]

Ken Nevadomi, whether he expresses his outrage with the brashness of comic strip color or social and psychological factors like police blotter reports, creates from things he knows or sees around him. His "stream of consciousness imagery" is a "rough expression of the bruised idealist." Nevadomi has been the most influential of a generation of painters (Douglas Max Utter and Pat Zinsmeister Parker among them) who "brought the expressive brush back into painting and he reinvigorated interest in the human figure."[45]

Craig Lucas paints imposing abstract compositions using rhythmically built-up, striated layers of paint on top of shapes. He blocks out geometric forms in a single color on the canvas; the shapes may be achieved by cutting or scraping away layers of paint applied earlier. The appearance is similar to an artist's color card. For Lucas there is a fusion of color and form skillfully developed by his painting process—of underpainting and building up the composition one layer

Craig Lucas, *Echo,* 1994, oil, wax, and flashe, 80" x 66". Courtesy of Progressive Corporation.

John Moore, *Bill*, 1989, oil on canvas, 66" x 78". Courtesy of Hahn Loeser & Parks LLP.

at a time until the viewer interacts with the results that excite and challenge. He uses squeegees and other devices to move the paint rhythmically and create the multilayered surfaces. Lucas is a former student and professor at Kent State University.[46]

John Moore, born in Cleveland, worked at General Motors before he focused on his education, receiving his BFA and MFA from Kent State University. He taught at Cuyahoga Community College and in the Art History and Education departments of the Cleveland Museum of Art. His painting *Bill* is representative of his abstract work. The smoothly painted dark oval shapes, almost human forms, seem as if they are moving across the space resembling a rough sea of contrasting uneven, aggressive brush strokes.

Patricia Zinsmeister Parker developed in the mid-1970s the elements that have become characteristic of her work over the years: abstract painting embellished with collage, eccentric and recognizable forms, and words. Her background as a greeting card designer and fashion illustrator is apparent as she signals the influence of ceramic and textile pattern.[47]

Shirley Aley Campbell uses painting to communicate—about the demise of the burlesque world or about the world of the derelict or about the bygone days of Euclid Beach. Campbell passionately records the human figure and its social context. Since the beginning of her career in the 1940s, her style has changed from figurative expressionism to total abstraction and, since the 1970s, from hard-edged realism toward a freer, more painterly realism, sometimes incorporating collage elements. The constant feature of her art has been superb drawing skills and commitment to life drawing. Campbell's art explores the vast range of the human condition. She paints strippers, celebrities, hookers, politicians, bullfighters, burlesque queens, alcoholics, and motorcyclists. Pursuing her subjects with the intensity of a reporter, she travels to observe people performing daily tasks in familiar surroundings, interviews them, and fills page after page with sketches. Despite the obvious opportunity for social or political commentary, she focuses on the common humanity of her subjects and presents each with individual compassion. Her work is devoted to the figure—drawn as she sees it as part of a design or composition—and as in most of her work, the figures overpower the canvas by visually extending beyond it.

Campbell grew her talent at the Cleveland Museum of Art and Cleveland Institute of Art. She shared her art with students at the Institute and at Cuyahoga Community College.[48]

Mary Lou Ferbert carries on Cleveland's legacy of watercolor. It is her sole medium. Neither the changing character of art nor new technologies have distracted her during this time. She teaches us to look until we see. A born Clevelander, her work examines her favorite subjects—the Flats, the beaches, the amusement parks, Cleveland Municipal Stadium, a lake freighter, Chester Commons, the West Side Market, and the Chagrin Falls Popcorn Shop—and focuses on "the interface of the natural and the engineered." The beauty and tension between the disparate elements is gently and gracefully persuasive in her large and strong, august and im-

Patricia Zinsmeister Parker, *Cuff-links*, 1990, diptych, latex enamel, oil, and cardboard on canvas, 74" x 136". Courtesy of Hahn Loeser & Parks LLP.

pressive paintings. A devout believer in the magic of her medium, Ferber says, "Watercolor makes my heart sing. The lyric quality as it flows from a charged brush; the record of the progress seen in the layered transparent washes; the potential for power, vitality and drama; the quiet gentleness: these attributes captivated me years ago and my enthusiasm has never waned."[49]

Drawing

During discussions of the region's Creative Essence, there were a number of participants who mourned the loss of drawing—the "handmade artwork." It was the "feel" of the expression, they said, the human component that we were losing with the advent of the huge role of computer graphics and composition. As Shirley Aley Campbell put it, "It is the bareness of drawing that I like, the act of drawing is what locates, suggests, discovers."[50]

Left: Shirley Aley Campbell, *Per Carnum*, 2004, oil, 30" x 40".

Right: Mary Lou Ferbert, *Old Door*, 1993, transparent watercolor, 85" x 41½".

Laurence Channing came to Cleveland in 1985 to head the Publications Department at the Cleveland Museum of Art. In addition to his important role in the region as an arts administrator, he has also become one of the area's leading artists. Channing uses the midwestern urban environment as the subject for his drawings. As one critic said, he draws "the authentic city . . . and reminds us that it is the authentic city, grown from years of use and abuse, that is the setting for the life of the mind." He begins his process by taking dozens of color photographs of a site; he abstracts elements, plays with perspective, and creates intriguing black and white compositions. He grinds charcoal in a mortar and applies it with various tools he makes from sticks and rags.[51]

Multimedia

At the end of the century it was usual to find painters who moved with ease from printmaking to painting and even to sculpture. There are so many materials and media and technologies to choose from, computers being but only one. There are muralist-photographers-painters, muralists-sculptors, and photographers-

Laurence Channing, *North Light,* 2001, image, 4½" x 4½", 14" x 15" paper, charcoal on Reeves BFK. Courtesy of Diane Schaffstein.

printmakers-craftspersons, and at one moment in a single exhibit the presentations sometimes include a single form, two forms, and multiple mixed media presentations.

Holly Morrison, best known as a photographer and printmaker, combines traditional methods of printmaking with new technologies, disclosing a connection between something established and something unpredictable. She is interested in how place informs perception and aspires to create work that moves the audience to reflect on the physical to the metaphysical. As her work has matured, we have had the opportunity to see Morrison's distinct creative patterns develop. Frequently

Holly Morrison, *The Golden Game,* 1997, painted ceiling and walls. Courtesy of Cleveland Public Library. Photograph by Don Snyder.

centering on the resolution of opposites, she has striven to dissipate arbitrary distinctions—between differing media, realism and abstraction, harmony and dissonance, external and internal, embodiment and intangibility. Like the alchemists she admires, Holly Morrison effects physical transformations which seem to radiate an aura of the spiritual.[52]

Michael Loderstedt, *Fairplay,* 1996, photography, hand-crafted boat with inscription, as exhibited at the Cleveland Museum of Art.

Don Harvey, *Bad Water*, 1991, photograph on aluminum, steel, and rubber, 74" x 84" x 3". Courtesy of Cleveland Museum of Art, gift of Mr. and Mrs. Richard A. Zellner.

Don Harvey was trained as a painter but has worked primarily in creating multimedia works that incorporate photography and sculptural elements. Harvey, who lived in Akron and along the Cuyahoga River, is most influenced by the industrial landscape and waterways—the grit and debris, the eeriness and loneliness. Harvey's use of steel and rubber make such sense relating to his art and teaching life in the region, and his commitment to making the relationship between the artist and the city exciting has been felt in his role in the development of SPACES, Inc and Cleveland Public Art.[53]

Michael Loderstedt has long been interested in photography, and it has become a major element in his paintings, prints, drawings, sculptures, photographs, handmade books, and installations. His work has been included in two seminal exhibits at the Cleveland Museum of Art: the 1996 invitational exhibit "Urban Evidence" and the 1999 "Cleveland Collects." He has taught in Kent State University's School of Art since 1989.[54]

Cleveland's Diversity

While all artists are "image gatherers" from their personal experience, their artistic heritage, their media, their fellow artists, and their society, there are groups of artists who have made their cultural heritage a central tenet of their art making.

Beyond the excellent mentoring at Karamu House, the strong curriculum at East and West Technical High Schools, the all-inclusive May Show at the Cleveland Museum of Art, the WPA program, and the projects and activities of the Cleveland Print Makers were the seminal exhibits of the Cleveland Artists Foundation: "Yet Still We Rise: African American Art in Cleveland, 1920–1970" (1996) and "Hungarians at the Easel" (2003). These exhibits explored the plurality of the region's art, which has always been present but is not usually mentioned. The exhibits focused on the artistic contributions of particular ethnic and national groups within the region.

The question of how, and if, artists of various ethnic groups reflect their culture in their work is a good, and frequently discussed, one. Many simply want to be recognized as artists and integrated into the fabric of regional and American art. Others want to be valued for their work and select subjects that emblazon their ethnic heritage. Indeed, some of the most substantial work by regional artists must be recognized for statements of heritage.

Charles Sallee, the oldest of fourteen children, was born in Oberlin and grew up in Sandusky. The son of a craftsman, a plasterer for public buildings and then the owner of his own construction firm, Sallée was the first African American to graduate from the Cleveland School of Art (now the Cleveland Institute of Art). He worked for the Works Progress Administration from 1936 to 1941 and was commissioned to do several murals in the Cleveland area at schools and hospitals (which, sadly, no longer exist; but one at Outwaithe Homes has been restored). After his service in WWII as a supervising draftsman for the corps of engineers, he concentrated on his portraits, life drawings, and still lifes, made in a sensitive, realistic style. He also supported himself as an interior designer for Cleveland-area restaurants, bars, and hotels, most notably Stouffers Inn-on-the Square in downtown Cleveland.[55]

Malcolm Brown creates landscapes that blur line and form to produce an atmospheric magic. A nationally recognized watercolorist, Brown has been working and teaching in the Cleveland area throughout his career. Working in soft colors with a loose stroke, Brown's work is at times abstract and at other moments evocative of scenes of city life. Although he is especially stimulated by the unending challenges of watercolor, he has used acrylic paints and mixed media as well. Brown and his wife, Ernestine, have brought local and nationally recognized African American artists to the attention of this region through the Malcolm Brown Gallery they established in 1980. His joins the heritage that is at once Romare Bearden in some of its universal urban subject matter or the heritage that is the best of the American Scene painters.[56]

Sandor Vago painted portraits as well as scene paintings. After studying in art academies in Budapest and Munich, and launching his artistic career in Budapest, Vienna, and Venice, he came to Cleveland in 1921. He participated in the art scene immediately, joining the Cleveland Society of Artists, opening a studio and developing a thriving career as a portrait painter and, also, as a teacher at the Cleveland School of Art from 1929 to 1935. And while his self-portraits are among his best works, his paintings of Hungarian peasant scenes identify his heritage. His style is expressive and painterly.

Michelangelo Lovelace, entrepreneurial and driven, exhibits his murals, paintings, and sculptures in the city's downtrodden neighborhood environments. The

theme of his work is community, and it addresses concerns about cultural, racial, and economic tensions in the inner city and reflects the life of the African American today. His paintings are compelling, invigorating, lively, and thoughtful.[57]

Angelica Pozo, born of Cuban and Puerto Rican parents in New York City, has lived in Cleveland since 1984. A full-time self-employed artist, Angelica divides her time between her widely exhibited sculptural studio work, her major public art commissions, and artist residencies involving large ceramic tile/mosaic projects primarily in arts-in-education programs. Her work deals "visually and thematically . . . with the natural world, landscape, plant forms, and speaks of femininity, sensuality and the development of my spiritual awareness." Her background training in ceramics, a medium steeped with a functionally based tradition, has given her the basis for her approach to public art. She cocreated with Penny Rakoff at Jacobs Field *Market Place/MeetingPlace: An Urban Memorial,* a short resting bench on the plaza. Rakoff researched the history and the accompanying photographs to be inserted into the design, and Angelica created the mosaic tiles of the fruits and vegetables that symbolize the Central Street Market that was demolished when Jacobs Field was built.[58]

Douglas Phillips determined he would be an artist early on. He developed his drawing and portrait skills in an outstanding high school art department in Buffalo,

Left: Malcolm Brown, *Jazz Messengers,* 1998, ceramic tile, 8' x 6'. Courtesy of Malcolm Brown Gallery.

Right: Sandor Vago, *Self-Portrait,* 1937, oil on canvas, 32¼" x 28". Courtesy of Cleveland Museum of Art, presented by the Friends of the Artist.

Above: Michelangelo Lovelace, *Born Again*, 2000, mural at 36th Street and Cedar Avenue.

Right: Angelica Pozo and Penny Rakoff, *Market Place/ Meeting Place: An Urban Memorial*, 1994, mosaic tile bench with photographic decals and historic artifacts, 18' x 25' x 7'. Photograph by Don Snyder.

at the Cleveland Institute of Art during WWII, and through advanced study at Syracuse University. When he returned to Cleveland, where his father lived, he reestablished contacts and joined John W. Winterich and Associates, a studio specializing in church interiors and where he helped set up the stained-glass department. He became persuaded by the "visceral" and powerful, not just visual, beauty of stained glass and made it his primary expression. He was one of the first to experiment with faceted glass, devising a method to include enameled (painted and fired) details. He was not only a good craftsman; he was a superb artist. His work shines in churches of all denominations all over the world. An African American, he felt a special freedom in designing for black churches, where his most flamboyant improvisations are almost like visual jazz, and his portrait studies for these churches are among his strongest and most dignified.[59]

Above: Douglas Phillips, *Christ Called Mankind,* 1991, stained-glass window. Courtesy of Messiah Lutheran Church. Photograph by Mona Phillips.

Left: Douglas Phillips, *Burning Bush,* 1961, stained-glass screen. Courtesy of Agodath B'nai Israel. Photograph by Mona Phillips.

The Artists, Past and Present 97

Cleveland's Artistic Institutions: Museums, Schools, Galleries, and Other Collections

It is important in any history of civilization to discuss those who have been supporters of the arts. During the Renaissance the church and city-state were the patrons of the artists. Almost every artist whose name we know today has work displayed in the churches or public buildings that were once homes of state leaders. The popes and nobility joined and even led the belief that art was an important human endeavor and that civilized society should support and honor individual talent. Over time, and with the emergence of the new urban middle class, merchants and industrialists provided patronage of artistic endeavor as a mantle of their civility. Today, patronage in terms of support for artists comes in many ways. With geographically and culturally diverse audiences, institutions and organizations have recognized that they can no longer stand alone as arbiters and sentries of art and culture. Their very survival is dependent on including like-minded organizations and the wider community in their programs and in their planning.

According to arts historian Margaret Lynch, "The fuller story of Cleveland cultural institutions—when and how they came to be founded, how they were supported and administered, and what tastes prevailed—has much to say about the distinctiveness of Cleveland's cultural growth in an American and particularly Midwestern context. It is not just a story of wealthy patrons, but also of arts administrators, artists, and the general public." The characteristics she identifies as having built the cultural strength of this region include leadership with a confident and diverse economic base, involvement in civic and governmental affairs, formal and informal settings for accomplishing business and fun, and a strong economic base that could bolster the arts, in turn spawning great civic pride.[1]

Arts and civic entrepreneurship at the turn of the twentieth century involved people of wealth whose models for this region's institutions came from other cities. In order to complete the vision of a city leading in industry, there needed to be museums and concert halls. And so the industrial leaders saw to it that these institutions were created. Katharine Lee Reid, CMA director, said, "I don't think that there's anywhere else in the world that has a great university, a natural history museum, an art institute with studio art programs and advanced degrees, music institutes, a botanical garden, and a world-renowned art museum that has benefited more from the foresight of its founders. Our founders recognized that you did not only need to have an economically successful city; you needed to have something where people tended to be taken out of the everyday world of commerce, and making money and into the realm of the spirit."[2]

When the wealth of these families diminished during the late 1920s and through the Depression, art was supported by the federal WPA artist employment program, which set in motion arts activity of unprecedented density and variety. Its major presence in this region was due to the leadership of William Millikin, director of the Cleveland Museum of Art. With the explosion of pop culture in the 1950s and 1960s, and a search for values and meaning to fill what has been characterized as a "spiritual vacuum," the U.S. Congress supported legislation that created the National Endowment for the Arts and, on its heels, fifty state arts councils, changing life for all of the arts thereafter. The years have seen ebb and flow, various arts and political issues under fire, but once-elite institutions started to search for broad audiences, community inclusion, and new sources of financial stability.

Major Institutions

The major visual arts institutions—those that have been in existence for most of the twentieth century—are still the mainstay of the region's art reputation. The museums have become stronger and more respected for their vigor and integrity. The Cleveland Public Library, newly renovated and expanded, has received and preserved ongoing important regional collections of works on paper and commissioned major regional work for the 1999 Louis Stokes wing. The Cleveland Institute of Art entered the new century with strong vision and imaginative leadership. The faculties of the colleges and university art departments have matured and produced a growing body of artwork of quality and students to nurture.

These institutions have their discrete missions, but each feels it is part of their mandate to partner with regional arts organizations in appropriate and relevant ways. As Mitchell Kahan, director of the Akron Art Museum, commented, "We all have a mantra about our work. Collaboration, collaboration, collaboration. There is no other way to operate these days. Involvement with other institutions, other disciplines, increases the perspective, the reach, the impact of every institution."[3]

University Circle has served as a unifying symbol: the Cleveland Museum of Art partners with Case Western Reserve University and the Cleveland Institute of Art; their curators have joint appointments, and the museum has several affiliated groups. Both the Cleveland Museum of Natural History and the Western Reserve

Allen E. Cole, *Call and Post Newsboys*, undated, photograph. Courtesy of the Western Reserve Historical Society.

Historical Society also have significant collections of regional art that are compatible with their missions. At the Cleveland Museum of Natural History there are ongoing exhibitions focused on nature, and the Western Reserve Historical Society focuses on work that is of regional historical significance, one example of which is the important collection of Allen Cole's photographic work acquired by the African American Archives. This collection of nearly 30,000 negatives, 6,000 original prints, 4 16mm films, and one oil painting summarizes this artist's style and impact as a documenter of the people and activities of the African American community during the twentieth century.

Cleveland Museum of Art

The founders of the Cleveland Museum of Art gave with a special civic stewardship. Henry Hurlbut, John Huntington, and Horace Kelley each left money to found a great art museum. But brought together by the foresighted Jeptha Wade, their benefactions worked together to build a single art museum that would benefit the whole city, region, and world. The CMA's outstanding and comprehensive collection, designed by its curators, grew out of the endowments that allowed for the ongoing purchase of great works of art by professionals who brought their skills to bear in the methodical and selective acquisitions of uniformly fine works of art from antiquity to the present.

In addition to its fine collection, the museum was the primary sponsor of the May Show, a most important force in this region's arts history. Like many urban

Left: Willard Combes, *Annual Exhibition of Cleveland Artists and Craftsmen of the Western Reserve, or The May Show,* ca. 1940, ink on illustration board, 16½" x 13¾". Courtesy of Cleveland Artists Foundation, gift of Jean Combes.

Right: John Clague, *Progression in Black and White,* 1963, black-and-white painted steel, 68'. Courtesy of Cleveland Museum of Art, the Wishing Well Fund.

art communities around the country at the turn of the century, Cleveland's artists formed groups to share, invent, and grow. One of the first of these groups was the Cleveland Art Association, formed to help and support local artists through exhibits and patronage. In 1915 the association proposed to the Cleveland Museum of Art that it hold an annual, broad-based exhibit featuring the spectrum of fine and applied arts. The exhibit, first held in 1919 and titled "The Cleveland Exposition of Artists and Craftsmen," became the model for the May Shows that graced the regional arts scene until the early 1990s.

The May Show had a strong influence on artists and collectors. Its power lay in four elements: the museum, the artists and craftspersons, the jury, and the visitors and patrons. An annual juried community event, tens of thousands of people attended to see the work of artists from the Cleveland region who had been invited to exhibit. These annual exhibits revealed and clarified regional trends and distinction in painting, photography, ceramics, textile, enamel, glass, jewelry, or metalwork. After World War II the May Show became an important and vital sales venue for Cleveland art. It was the one place where the artist could meet his or her public, and because the shows were juried, inclusion in the show was a stamp of approval.

In almost every public discussion on the Cleveland art scene, the demise of the May Show emerges and is lamented. The May Shows represented a sense of community and a sharing that was felt deeply by the generations that participated.

The Northeast Ohio Show—NEO—reinvigorates the museum's rich tradition of celebrating the artists of northeastern Ohio with a special juried exhibition dedicated to their work.

The museum's plans for the future include an expansion by internationally renowned architect Rafael Vinoly that will include restoration of the original 1916 beaux arts building as well as the 1971 Marcel Breuer annex. These renovations and expansions will increase temporary exhibition space as well as make more room available for showing a greater number of selections from the permanent collection of more than 40,000 objects and works. There will be a spacious public lobby and more classroom accommodations for focused educational purposes.

Cleveland Public Library

The Cleveland Public Library (CPL) is another of our major arts institutions. Since its inception in 1869, its collections and buildings have included sculptures, murals, tiles, and decorative arts using themes from classic to current times. Significant is its major collection of works on paper from the New Deal art projects. Linda Eastman, CPL director from 1918 to 1938, the only woman to head a large metropolitan library at the time, was a strong supporter of the WPA federal arts projects. She was convinced that the visual arts were as instructional and inspirational as the written word.[4]

The public library is the memory point of a city. Cleveland's is the third largest public research library in our nation, and among its peers (like the New York Public Library and the Boston Public Library) it is highly respected for its international holdings, which are impressive in quality and in quantity. Its collection of more than one million photographs is growing. It has a more extensive collection of this region's art than any other institution outside of the museum, gathering pieces by gift, donation, and purchase. As with most public collections, the library's can be divided into two distinct areas. The first is art commissioned by, or given to, the library with the intention that it will always be on display to the public. Often this is commemorative art, which celebrates an event or a person. The second includes the art that is bought by or donated to the library, thus becoming part of its subject collections. This art is only occasionally displayed, usually only during special events or exhibits, and is viewed mostly by researchers.[5] In addition to WPA prints, artist's studies, architects' drawings, and other works on paper, murals and ceilings capture the attention of all who walk into these wonderful buildings.

From 1979 until 1985 the library completed a huge construction and renovation of eighteen branch library buildings. Local architects were invited to submit proposals that uniquely conceptualized the library's program statements and the distinguishing character of the neighborhood branch building. Similarly, the CPL integrated regional artwork into its branches. Malcolm Brown's *Jazz Messengers,* a colorful mosaic tile mural on the exterior entrance wall of the Langston Hughes branch on Superior Avenue, reflects the past glory of jazz along East 105th Street, and other examples of local artists' work gracing the library's branches include an abstract painting by Andrea Hahn, a silkscreen print by Eugenie Torgeson, and a copper owl by William McVey.[6]

A process for selecting public art solidified in recent times for this region with the work of the Committee for Public Art (now Cleveland Public Art). Since 1984 this organization has been dedicated to raising the aesthetic goals and establishing the finest professional standards in creating exciting places in Cleveland's urban landscape by acting as a vehicle for collaboration between artists and design professionals. An independent, nonprofit organization, it has been a catalyst for bringing excellent artistic talent to civic projects in neighborhoods, commercial districts, and beloved public spaces while inspiring the public to imagine and participate in the process. Its public art projects resonate: the Bicentennial Bridge Lighting, Gateway, Jacobs Field, the Cleveland Public Library, the Detroit-Superior Bridge pedestrian promenade, and the Euclid Corridor Public Art master plan.

Cleveland Institute of Art

At the heart of Cleveland's art scene is the Cleveland Institute of Art (CIA). Opened in 1882 as the Western Reserve School of Design for Women with a principal, one student, and founder Sarah M. Kimball, 120 years later more than 600 students graduate as competitive gallery artists, product and transportation designers, graphic designers, photographers, contemporary craftsmen, and educators.

The school's origins trace back to 1875, when Archibald Willard, Otto Bacher, Frederick Gottwald, and others formed the Cleveland Art Club and met on the top floor of City Hall and sponsored art exhibits and classes. Mostly of German origin, they called themselves "the Old Bohemians." While the French Barbizon School and European romantic traditions were popular in the nineteenth century, even in the United States, the Old Bohemians were influenced more by their training in Munich and Dusseldorf and worked with firm definitions of mass and planes and in a darker, murkier palette. In turn, this group of artists had a profound, and long-lived, effect on their students, who became this region's next generation of artists.

By the late 1800s Cleveland was reaping the benefits of its position in the Industrial Age and the fortunes made from decades of canal and railroad construction, allowing these successful industrialists and entrepreneurs to turn their attention to objects of beauty for their homes. Up to this time, with a few exceptions, wealthy Clevelanders bought their paintings in other American cities or in Europe.

In 1878 a large and successful exhibition sponsored by a group of leading Cleveland women brought together hundreds of works from private collectors in the region and elsewhere. The "Home Art" part of the exhibit featured work by Cleveland artists and gave attention to the talent here at home. The exhibit was the basis for the development of the Western Reserve School of Design. The 1883 prospectus by the school stated that "while we may be glad to foster and develop the fine arts, our first care is for the art industries. . . . America should be able to compete with Europe with its industries—such as glass painting, china decorating, pottery and the like—all of which tends greatly to increase the wealth and importance of a country.[7]

The first years were dominated by discussions over what to teach and whether the school should be independent or merge with Western Reserve University. It stayed independent and in 1891 became the Cleveland School of Art, with a curriculum balanced to teach the fine and applied arts. From the start, men and women formed the student body, with initial goals being to place women in jobs such as designing for window shade companies and dry goods and home furnishings companies producing curtains and carpets. Indeed, the women graduates established a good reputation quickly and replaced outsourcing to New York for the work at the dry goods company Baldwin, Hatch and Company.

The school outgrew the old City Hall attic space it shared with the Art Club (where a leaky roof forced students to work under umbrellas), and in 1892 both groups moved to the estate of Horace Kelley, who managed properties in the city and on North Bass Island in Lake Erie. Upon his death, Kelley bequested land to "build a school or college for designing, drawing, painting and other fine arts," which caused some tension in the arts scene. Both the club and school lobbied for the money, but in the end the school was chosen to receive the property, which they put to good use—from the attic where Gottwald taught his life classes to the stables where Louis Rorimer held his clay-modeling classes. In 1904 the Cleveland School of Art moved into its new home on the land Jeptha Wade had donated in Wade Park, and "The First Annual Exhibition of Cleveland Artists," which included painters, craftsmen, and sculptors, was held there in 1906.

Through the years the Cleveland School of Art grew, adding a clay-modeling studio for Herman Matzen, establishing a Department of Commercial Illustration headed by Henry Keller, and appointing talented faculty to fill teaching roles. By its thirtieth anniversary the school had shown its potential and had added summer and Saturday-morning classes to educate the public about the power of the arts. Indeed, it had become one of the leading art schools in the country. Cleveland's industrial leaders, who supported the school generously, recognized that the arts here were gaining national attention and deemed it time for an art museum.

During the 1920s the school was overcrowded. But following the Crash of 1929, plans for expansion were scratched. While faculty and staff were significantly reduced during the Depression years, there were some key appointments made: R. Guy Cowan in Ceramics, Viktor Schreckengost in Industrial Design, and Edris Eckhardt in Ceramics. But real growth in faculty and student aid didn't come until after World War II. During the war courses were offered to support the war effort, including mapmaking, camouflage design, scientific and medical drawing, and occupational therapy.

In 1946–47 one-third of the student body of 485 was veterans studying under the GI Bill; 700 more attended evening and Saturday classes. Classes were held twelve months a year. Space was rented to accommodate the classes, and there was a reorganization of the curriculum. Goals were set to raise the standards of achievement. The Department of Sculpture was expanded, and there were new opportunities for those interested in creative work in metals and jewelry making as well as ceramics and ceramic design. It was at this time that the school name was changed to the Cleveland Institute of Art to reflect its image as a training center for professional artists. It was now seen as a place where there was a connection between the artistic process and innovation, where new ideas in design, technique, and function could be tested and critiqued.

In 1955 Joseph McCullough became the first alumnus to be appointed director of the Institute, and in 1956 the present East Boulevard facility opened with an envisioned capacity of 400 students. For the first time there was proper library space with a media center for slides, tapes, and audio-visual equipment. One of McCullough's goals was to provide academic study in order to qualify for regional accreditation. During the 1960s a full complement of faculty members was added to teach the humanities and social sciences; and the fifth-year BFA program became a requirement for all students, the only such program in the country.

Under the leadership of president David Deming (1998–), another alumnus and an active sculptor, the Institute developed an expansion plan to move the school into the new technology age and to better serve the students and the community in the twenty-first century. Students can select courses from a new Digital Arts major, that includes video installations, performance art, film, sound, animation, web design, and multimedia productions. Visual Culture, another new major, incorporates competencies in cross-cultural understanding, critical theory and methods of analysis, contemporary arts issues, popular/mass culture, new media and philosophy, and aesthetic theories and criticism.

The Akron Art Museum

The Akron Art Museum, the leading museum of modern art in northeast Ohio, has come a long way since its founding in 1922. First known as the Akron Art Institute, it occupied two rooms in the basement of the Akron Public Library on East Market Street. These rooms served the institute for ten years, until library expansion forced it out in 1932. Thereafter, the institute was housed in a variety of locations until the City of Akron offered the entire former library building at 69 East Market Street—where the institute had first resided. In 1950 the city celebrated the opening of the new facility, its home for the next thirty-one years.

In 1974 the institution's board of trustees decided to specialize the collection and exhibitions, formalizing an approach that had begun in the late 1960s, and establish specific new goals. Emphasizing the best in regional, national, and international visual arts, the collection would focus on the finest art from 1850 to the present. To reflect its new mission of collection and preserving, exhibiting and educating, the Akron Art Institute became known in 1981 as the Akron Art Museum and moved into the renovated turn-of-the-century post office directly across the street.

The basic strengths of the museum's collection lie in three areas. The oldest works are part of the Edwin C. Shaw Collection (one of the museum's founders): thirty-four turn-of-the-century American paintings, including works by William Merritt Chase, George Inness, and Childe Hassam. The second strength is in American painting and sculpture since 1960. Since the mid-1970s, the museum had added important works to its contemporary collection by artists such as Frank Stella, Chuck Close, Donald Judd, Andy Warhol, Helen Frankenthaler, Philip Guston, Claes Oldenburg, and Richard Deacon. A third specialty is their photographic collection. Although some important works date from the Civil War period, the collection focuses on the twentieth century, with images by Alfred Stieglitz and Ansel Adams spanning the early decades and Diane Arbus, Harry Callahan, Robert Frank, Gilbert and George, and Carrie Mae Weems as part of the contemporary works. An exhibition program of regional, national, and international interest has included comprehensive as well as smaller, diverse shows obtained from distinguished museum and private collections. The museum's education programs include lectures, gallery talks, poetry, film, jazz concerts, artist workshops, and cultural festivals.

Since its humble beginnings, the Akron Art Museum has played an increasingly vital role in Akron. Continuing in that tradition, the museum is poised to make history with its new 65,000-square-foot building designed by world-renowned architecture firm Coop Himmelb(l)au. The dynamic, soaring structure will be built adjacent to the existing museum, effectively incorporating the new into the old.

Public Art

Art situated in public places assumes a special role in the life of a community or city. After beaux arts and WPA, following a midcentury trend in blank-walled buildings, we (and nearly every other city) recognized the importance of ornament and decoration and missed it. City committees for public art and funding—which included art experts, public agency representatives, local and regional artists, interested citizens—were established to not only raise money but to review the design process.

Cleveland's cultural property includes some 250 sculpture pieces in Cuyahoga County and more than sixty in the City of Cleveland—at intersections, at Rockefeller Park, at the Cleveland Zoo, outside of corporate buildings, outside and inside public buildings—all of which contribute to our intellectual, artistic, historic, and social environment.

The legacy of public art in Cleveland resides in City Hall, where more than a hundred years ago the first artists' studios were located. However, the City of Cleveland has never included public art in their civic vision. While city planners did

Carl Floyd, *Tempus Pons,* 1984–85, sculpture, 1,000 ceramic tiles on stone and concrete, Ohio Arts Council Art in Public Places Project. Courtesy of City of Cleveland. Photograph by William Pinter.

help find a place for Claes Oldenburg's *Free Stamp* after it lost its original site in front of the BP America building on Public Square, and we can point to the restoration of the Marshall Frederick sculpture on the Mall as another example of interest, there has not been an ongoing concern for new public art or maintaining the traditional art. While the City Council had some interest, the mayors of Cleveland buried the idea for thirty years. Building legislation introduced in 1975 and 1985 in City Council would have mandated up to 2 percent of the cost of public buildings be allocated for artwork, including maintenance—a law similar to those passed in hundreds of cities, large and small. Finally, in 2003, legislation passed requiring 1.5 percent of the construction budget for each new municipal project or improvement project go to the design, creation, and placement of art, with the city assuming administrative and art maintenance costs and responsibility. The projects are seen as community development tools and will involve the public; a public art committee will advise the planning commission throughout the process.

Cleveland Public Art (CPA), organized as the Committee for Public Art in 1985, was formed to make art an integral part of the development of the city's "people places." Among its accomplishments, it had an integral role in building and "decorating" the library's Louis Stokes wing and in assisting in the development of the public process for the designs for the RTA Waterfront Rapid Transit Stops and in coordinating site-specific art for Jacobs Field.

There is historic precedent for decorated facades in Western architecture, and even more so in other traditions, dating to the earliest eras. The material itself may provide pattern and aesthetic interest, or the frieze-work may be an integral part of the building design. Some of the most interesting regional friezes go back to WPA days when several of the Cuyahoga Metropolitan Housing Authority buildings included exterior stone sculpture built into the architecture. Of special note, and having received national attention, are the works of Viktor Schrekengost during the 1950s: at the Cleveland Zoo, where five large sculptures on the bird building portray the development of birds from prehistoric times and a relief of pachyderms is displayed on the pachyderm building; and at Lakewood High School,

Viktor Schreckengost, *Early Settler*, 1955, ceramic terra-cotta sculpture, 18' x 34'. Photograph by Berni Rich.

Max Kalish, *Abraham Lincoln,* 1932, bronze statue. Reprinted with permission of Don Kalish and the Sculpture Center.

William McVey, *Tom Johnson,* 1987, bronze sculpture on granite base. Courtesy of Case Western Reserve University. Photograph by the Sculpture Center.

where he placed a terra-cotta sculpture of colored glazes in earth tones, blue, yellow, and red titled *Early Settler.* (The zoo's bird building was demolished, but the tiles were stored for future use.) In modern times, rarely are exterior artworks developed as an initial part of building plans. Individuals, artists, architects, or owners—either by self-initiated interest or through approaches by interested people or organizations— initiate the plans. Motives may vary, but they usually spring from a desire to create interest in the building and the activities within or to cover a dirty wall. (Examples include Mark Howard's colorful mural on the Cleveland School of the Arts building and Michelangelo Lovelace's *Born Again* painted façade on an old building at 36th and Cedar.)

Public sculptures take meaning from their context, which is often altered, diluted, or enhanced without regard for the effect on the work of art. Once these works have outlived their patrons, their future depends on their ability to attract new audiences who will find their stories compelling and their messages meaningful.

Viewers and owners of public sculpture assume that these works will last forever because they are created from a substantial material like bronze or stone rather than canvas, paper, paint, or pencil. However, time has shown that maintenance of this public art is a necessary process and an important issue. The Sculpture Center, founded in 1989, completed the conservation of sculptures of General Moses Cleveland and Tom L. Johnson for Cleveland's bicentennial year and then tackled the Luke Easter Monument, Jesse Owens Olympic Champion, Ideal Boy Scout, and the Hugh O'Neill Memorial statues. In each of the subsequent years, single works and sculpture groups have been restored and renewed. Regardless of media, outdoor sculpture is susceptible to pollution, vandalism, and neglect, but with proper care outdoor sculpture can maintain its beauty.

The Medicis of the 1980s and 1990s

Corporate patronage of the arts took shape in the 1980s. All over the country, these modern-day Medicis—corporations, law offices, banks, health institutions—began to reexamine their work environment and understand the benefits of having art collections. The Progressive Insurance Company, whose collection actually preceded this movement, is one of the top corporate collections in the country. It includes fine provocative and cutting-edge paintings, works on paper, photography,

Lilian Tyrrell, *Poisonous Legacy,* 1990, tapestry, linen and silk, 58' x 117". Courtesy of Progressive Corporation.

and sculpture done by emerging artists working locally, nationally, and internationally. There is no central theme to the collection; it is an ongoing exploration of artistic expression. Based on the premise that the art on the walls changes you whether you know it or not, and that people grow and learn from it, this collection is intended to be controversial.

A unique example of a law firm showcasing this region's art has been built with the idea of establishing a cohesive collection, one with intellectual validity. Started in the late 1970s, the collection at Hahn, Loeser & Parks LLP numbers more than eighty works and focuses on Ohio and this region's artists. The works honor the legacy of Cleveland School artists such as Henry Keller, August Biehle, Clara Deike, and Frank Wilcox as well as pieces from the geometric abstraction period by David Davis, John Pearson, and Edwin Mieczkowski. Richard Zellner, the retired partner who curated the collection, notes that "the challenge is to hang pieces in a coherent learning environment, making people think about their environment, make it adventuresome and available to employees, clients, and visitors."[8] Perhaps one of the most powerful pieces in this collection is Mark Howard's *Third Precinct.*

The Standard Oil Corporation began to collect artwork in the 1980s as a means of enlivening the workplace and providing a stimulating atmosphere for its employees. The collection, which contained more than 1,200 pieces, featured much

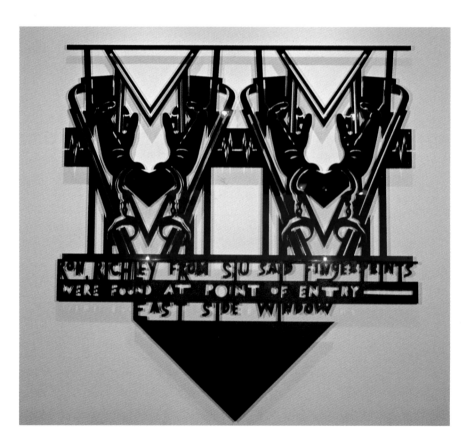

Mark Howard, *Third Precinct*, 1996, laser-cut mirrored Plexiglas on painted wood panel (with text found in a police station), 76" x 75". Courtesy Hahn Loeser & Parks LLP.

Judith Salomon, *Platters,* 2000. Courtesy of University Hospitals Chagrin Headlands Medical Center.

work by regional artists so as to reflect the company's commitment to the community. There were staff dedicated to programs of exhibition, loan, and art education, which included their work with the Corporate Art Club and the Committee for Public Art in giving tours of downtown sculpture sites. When British Petroleum acquired Standard Oil and its subsidiaries, including manufactories Chase Brass of Cleveland and Carborundum Company of Niagara Falls, the company deaccessioned some of the art. When BP closed its Chase offices in Solon in 1990, it gave the collection of Chase's brass and chrome-plated art deco–style artworks to the Western Reserve Historical Society to preserve this piece of Cleveland's industrial manufacturing history. Similarly, after BP sold the business assets of the Carborundum Company, a maker of ceramic tiles and industrial abrasives, the company's distinguished ceramic collection assembled by the company was authenticated and exhibited at the Cleveland Museum of Natural History, giving it a pre-Columbian collection unrivaled in our region.[9] The nearly 300 works of art that remain in the BP collection continue to enliven the work environment of company employees, who have had a say in their placement.

University Hospital also maintains a collection, which is financed by the hospital's Fine Arts Fund and is spread throughout more than 110 facilities. Trudy Wiesenberger, who serves as curator of the collection, sets standards and gives the impetus for finding a way of helping people understand art. Other health facilities with medium or large collections include the Cleveland Clinic, Akron Children's Hospital, and Kaiser Permanente, and all employ art consultants.

Fred Schmidt, *Freedom Dance,* 2000, painted metal, 44" x 23½" x 73½". Courtesy of Cleveland Clinic.

The region's collections, which number between fifty and a hundred, are in a variety of venues—law offices, banks, health facilities, educational facilities, and corporations—and vary in size from those with a handful of works to those with more than a thousand pieces. The important issues are the philosophic grounds for their development, the contents of the collections, the speed with which they are usually developed, and the skill that the art dealers have to bring to counsel their clients. What is disturbing is when, perhaps under new management or consolidation, a collection is relegated to corporate "inventory" with no one in charge of maintenance and oversight.

Organizations Blossom

The characteristics related to the establishment of the National Endowment of the Arts in 1965 came from the impetus of the so-called explosion of popular culture of the 1950s and the search for value and meaning in life. The presence of a spiritual vacuum seemed broad enough to support the further development of state and community arts councils. These agencies stimulated and still are evolving new ways to support the arts and artists. The Cleveland Area Arts Council (1972–79) was one of the country's citywide community councils, and its focus was on arts advocacy and education and service and programming for artists and arts organizations. Cleveland is still struggling with how to support fully its strong mix of artists and arts organizations.

Included in the mix of organizations that made this last twenty years of the century especially fertile are NOVA, SPACES, and the Cleveland Center for Contemporary Art (changed to Museum of Contemporary Art Cleveland in 2002). These groups are a few examples of nonprofit organizations that are generators and collaborators with the collecting institutions and are of major importance to the support picture for artists.

NOVA (New Organization for Visual Arts) came out of a 1972 forum on the state of the visual arts in the region sponsored by the Cleveland Area Arts Council. Artists expressed discontent with their conditions in that the only venue for seeing, evaluating, and buying their art seemed to be the May Show, sponsored by the Cleveland Museum of Art. For more than twenty-five years NOVA existed as a professional artists organization and was the hub of activity for 800 member-artists in the region. It brought together artists and art patrons through exhibits, a sales division (NOVART) for marketing to corporate clients, and an annual arts festival that featured exhibitions all over the city and a temporary major outdoor public installation. Another activity, Open Studio Days, offered a program of visitation to 200 artists studios. The Image Resource Center was a print workshop that, for the few years of its existence, was the center of cutting-edge computer-generated ad color copier artwork. Other NOVA projects included Art in Public Places, which brought art to malls, senior citizen homes, and schools, and assisting the Archives of American Art in the development of six films documenting the lives of area artists. In 1999, with a budget of $200,000 to $300,000 and a new generation of young and mature artists alike, all with different needs, NOVA artists and supporters agreed to disband, giving way to other organizations.

SPACES was begun in 1977 by a group of artists who wanted to present their work in the way they wanted it to be seen, creating an alternative to the commercial

Laila Voss, *A Chaotic Symphony: The Catch-All Net,* 1996, raw and recycled materials.

gallery scene or museums. These artists wanted control over their work and career. The group moved several times, first to the warehouse district (where many artists lived until it became high rent and trendy and unaffordable) before settling into its permanent home in a three-story warehouse on the near–West Side above the Flats. Thanks to an NEA Advancement Grant and matching local funds and generous help from friendly architects, volunteers, and other professionals, the artists renovated this space and opened three months after acquiring the property, making them one of the few "alternative" arts organizations in the nation that owns its own building. It has kept its focus, showing work by younger, emerging artists who experiment with new ideas. It is often the first exhibition venue for artists just out of graduate school or for artists who have never shown a major body of work anywhere. They take risks on new, unfamiliar work that challenges, often confronts, and that encourages discussion, debate, and interaction. This give-and-take allows for the possibility of change in the cultural landscape and helps us encounter art with an open mind. As an evidence of their involvement in the whole arts scene, they housed and helped found the Committee for Public Art (now Cleveland Public Art) and presented five exhibitions of charrettes for public art projects in collaboration with the committee and the RTA.

The Center for Contemporary Art began its historic roots in 1969 as the New Gallery. At that time it was a commercial gallery devoted to bringing cutting-edge art to Cleveland. Founded by Marjorie Talalay and Nina Sundell, the project was an experiment that had whetted the appetite of the local art scene. It did not, however, have enough buying power to sustain itself as a gallery, and by the 1970s it was transformed into a nonprofit organization. For the last thirty years it has retained its identity as a regionally based but nationally focused center for contemporary art. In the 1970s the New Gallery was in a storefront on Euclid Avenue and then in a converted house in University Circle; in 1991 the Center moved into

Joseph O'Sickey, *In the Garden,* 1972, oil, 62" x 48". Courtesy of Frances and Seth Taft. Photograph by Rob Muller.

its current space in the Cleveland Play House complex, thereby quadrupling its space. It presents special exhibitions of contemporary art—whether a solo exhibition, a group exhibition, photography, traditional painting and sculpture, or new mediums in installation or video art. In 2002 the Cleveland Center for Contemporary Art changed its name to Museum of Contemporary Art Cleveland. In deciding how it can best support contemporary regional artists and still balance that with the mission to present nationally recognized art here, the institution decided that small group or solo exhibitions would be especially advantageous to the artists.

The William Busta Gallery must be considered as well in the mix of support groups for regional artists. The gallery opened in 1989 in a Murray Hill storefront at a time when there were plenty of opportunities for artists to exhibit but few places where artists could count on having regular shows with ongoing representation. The intent at the Busta Gallery was to exhibit an artist's oeuvre as a coherent, substantial body of work. The single-person shows allowed a thorough look and gave audiences, patrons, critics, and other artists the opportunity to take full measure of each artist's capacity and achievement. The gallery mainly showed midcareer artists who lived and worked in northeast Ohio, among them Don Harvey, Michael Loderstedt, Douglas Max Utter, H. C. Cassill, and Karin Bartimole. For some artists, like Douglas Lucak, Kirk Mangus, Eva Kwong, Holly Morrison, Ray Juaire, Patty Fields, and Paul O'Keefe, even though they had exhibited extensively, the gallery wound up presenting their first one-person show in Cuyahoga County. Sadly, the gallery closed in 2001. The economies of the early century made it an uphill struggle to maintain the patrons and audience, and camaraderie and community, that had developed over ten years.

The Cleveland Artists Foundation, founded in 1984 to research, preserve, and exhibit the region's art, has produced four to five exhibits a year; published catalogs and monographs; sponsored programs, symposia, panels, and lectures; and maintianed a growing collection of 1,500 works. Its vision is to become a major center and resource for the public and the scholar alike.

There are also enterprises that have placed regional art at the forefront for a century, including the Vixeboxe Gallery, the Bonfoey Company, and Potter and Mellen. New vitality in galleries such as Art Metro and Headfooters bring fresh perspectives from regional artists. More recently established art dealers James Corcoran, Rachel Davis, and William Tregoning have discovered works never before seen and enlightened the community. And, certainly, we cannot forget the serious private collectors of regional art, among them Frances and Seth Taft, Elaine and Joseph Kisvardai, Joseph Erdelac, and Ann and Hugh Brown, whose deep interest in our own art and artists keeps the region's scene lively and vital.

Curators and scholars such as William Robinson, Tom Hinson, Henry Adams, and Ed Henning have organized our thinking about this region's art. And writers, including Jay Hoffman, Roger Welchans, Elizabeth McClellend, Ruth Dancyger, Rotraud Sackerlotsky, and Marianne Berardi, have written articles, catalogs, and monographs that clarify important pieces of the whole. Furthermore, another factor to mention is the impact of art criticism that developed regionally during the last years of the century. Publications like the multistate *New Art Examiner* and Ohio's *Dialogue* magazines offered readers announcements of statewide visual arts events and competitions, well-developed critiques, announcements of future exhibitions, and articles on arts issues, giving Clevelanders a good idea of what was happening and on what level. And it wasn't until the 1990s that the *Cleveland Plain Dealer* hired its first art critic (although reviewers such as Grace Kelly and Helen Borsick Cullinan had kept the community informed and lent support to regional artists and events throughout the century). In-depth articles by well-versed arts writers such as Steven Litt, Frank Green, Douglas Max Utter, Dan Tranberg, and Amy Sparks appeared in various publications, such as *Northern Ohio Live* magazine and the alternative *Free Times* newspaper, and churned community discussion.

Forging the Future

At each session of the Creative Essence series of dialogues, building an arts community was discussed. As an attempt is made to pull the parts of this discourse together, it seems instructive to look at the criteria used to identify the best small art towns in America as defined by John Villani,[1] which, with year-round populations of 65,000 or less, are attracting artists and culturally minded patrons, gallery owners, and festival promoters. Each has events, work spaces, bookstores, and hangouts. While it's possible to identify the similarities of these communties, each has distinctions that identify its locale—beauty of geography, environment, life-style, historic charm, quirkiness, the pastiche of population, renovated turn-of-the-century commercial buildings, "the solace of open spaces," and arts districts.

So, we wonder, does Cleveland have a place for interested public, artists, and collectors? Do we have a single place that offers an arts and cultural district, affordable housing, urban amenities, and the artists and their art? At the end of the century we were still sorting, and struggling with these issues of place. In the discussions of our own region, Cleveland-area artists expressed a need for "community" as they talked about a communal place for artists, while the public felt a need for "community" most often articulated as the kind of feeling generated by the May Show.

Lively public input from a variety of advisories, forums, and several significant formal studies gave the Community Partnership for Arts and Culture in the late 1990s the broad base of information and knowledge about the issues and identified the major challenges for individual artists who live in this region. Northeast Ohio's Arts and Culture Plan was developed by the Partnership for the regional community that has artists, arts, and cultural organizations at its center. A broad plan, it addresses access, education, partnerships, and resources for all of the arts and cultural organizations and individual artists of the region.[2]

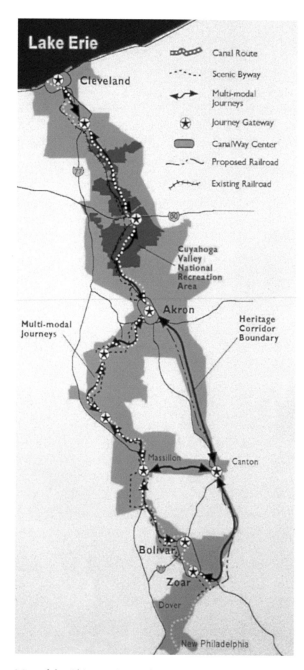

Map of the Ohio & Erie Canal National Heritage Corridor, 2000.

The preservation, restoration, and adaptive use of Cleveland's old buildings is another important issue. These spaces honor the past and stand ready for the future. Under any scrutiny, these are distinctive and distinguished models of quality in craftsmanship, engineering, and technology. The intent of the originators is preserved, their dreams incorporated and perhaps even surpassed. Organizations such as the Cleveland Restoration Society and the Sculpture Center have focused the community's awareness on the meaning and value of our historic buildings and artworks and expanded their mission to give technical assistance and guidance to the planning for preservation. This visionary process will be ensured with the help of the owners and an endowed maintenance fund. Along with Cleveland Public Art programs and publications, it educates and builds the next generations of conservationists.[3]

This area must also develop a deeper understanding of our roots. The Cuyahoga Valley National Park and all its potential development, corridors, towpaths, walking places, and meeting places summarize the regional community that we've inherited and share. It is possible that if things go in the direction they are envisioned, the Ohio & Erie Canal National Heritage Corridor, running 110 miles from Cleveland to New Philadelphia, will connect this densely populated northern urban center with less populated cities and rural communities. The finishing of the trail alone is seen as a spur to adaptive reuse of older buildings, construction of new buildings, environmental reclamation, and economic renewal for the region.

Northeast Ohio needs to take pride in the inheritance of an industrial past. This undeniable landscape is our region, and we must do something with it, be it creating a home for the remaining Hulett ore unloaders or understanding the viability of brownfield development. Artists have already attempted to do so, using images and materials of the landscape. We must seize opportunities to work with artists to bridge the gap between the old and new industries and under-

South facade of the Cleveland Museum of Art. Photograph by Jennie Jones.

stand what we are honoring, what we have inherited, and how technologies can help us remember them in meaningful ways.[4]

We must also help Cleveland better understand and appreciate its vital and expanding cultural institutions by supporting them as they act definitively and bravely and inspire us with their new buildings. These are, after all, the symbols of our culture.

But at the core are the artists—talented individuals of national and even international renown who call this northeast Ohio home. This is their base of creative power, the heart of their intellectual resuscitation, the stem cell of their work.

There are many younger talented artists and architects in our artistic community. Every once in a while we are swept away by their powerful message, perception, and thoughtful delivery. Some are emerging, some are growing, and some are maturing. Time will tell who will become the distinctive and distinguished artists of this new century.

In this region more small manufacturing parts are made than in any other region of the world; here polymer and biotechnology materials and research are embedded in our history and our future. We are not Boston, New York, Baltimore, or even Chicago, the nation's art meccas and cultural centers. Our relatives are Detroit, St. Louis, and Buffalo. William Busta said, "Cultural geographers say that we are one region that does not define ourselves as north, east, mid-west, south. Maybe that's a lack of identity, maybe that's the soul of the country. Art that is created here always reminds us that when we look at great art, art is not something that just happens someplace else. . . . It happens here as well, and it has meaning within our lives, and it has capacity to enter our hearts and souls and help us to define who we are."[5] We don't have to change who we are. We just have to understand ourselves and move with a spirit of forward thinking.

When architect, academic, and community arts leader Foster Armstrong reviewed the proposal for the dialogue series, he commented that the focus of this project on interconnections and reciprocal relations among culture, technology, and the arts in the region was a good introduction to our subject as long as we could "clearly and passionately interpret and convey our creative essence to others."[6] And I sincerely hope that is what we have been able to do.

Notes

Beginnings

1. David Young, "Ohio," in *Seasoning: A Poet's Year* (Columbus: Ohio State Univ. Press, 1999), viii–xi. Reprinted with permission of the author.

Our Regional Culture: Place, People, and Industry

1. William H. Gerdts, *Art across America: Two Centuries of Regionalist Painting* (New York: Abbeville, 1990), 212–25.

2. Charles Whittlesey's 400-page book of the history, archeology, and geology of the Cleveland area became a basic resource for all future documentation. Interestingly, Whittlesey served as the first president of the Western Reserve Historical Society, the oldest cultural institution in Cleveland. William C. Mills, *An Archaeological Atlas of Ohio* (Columbus: F. J. Heer, 1914); Tim Donovan, "Defining Region: Then and Now—Place, People, and Industry," Creative Essence dialogue, June 6, 2000, Western Reserve Historical Society.

3. Canal map, "Ohio Historic Canals," July 2004, Canal Society of Ohio, http//my.oh.voyager.net.

4. David Steinberg, "The Forest City Rises: Symbol and Value in Cleveland's First Pictures," in William Robinson and David Steinberg, *Transformations in Cleveland Art, 1796–1946: Community and Diversity in Early Modern America,* exhibition catalog (Cleveland: CMA, 1996), 28.

5. Gladys Haddad, "William Sommer, Henry Keller, Frank Wilcox," Interpreters of the Western Reserve Symposium, 1993; Sandy Reichert, ed., *Cleveland as a Center of Regional American Art* (Cleveland: Cleveland Artists Foundation, 1994); Rotraud Sackerlotzky, with an essay by O. P. Reed Jr., *August F. Biehle, Jr.: Ohio Landscapes,* ed. Ellen G. Landau, exhibition catalog (Cleveland: Case Western Reserve University, 1986); Rotraud Sackerlotzky and Mary Haverstock, *F. C. Gottwald and the Old Bohemians,* exhibition catalog (Cleveland: Cleveland Artists Foundation, 1993).

6. Rotraud Sackerlotzky, *Henry Keller's Summer School in Berlin Heights,* exhibition catalog (Cleveland: Cleveland Artists Foundation, 1990).

7. Holly Morrison, "The Artists, Past and Present," Creative Essence dialogue, Mar. 16, 2001, Cleveland Institute of Art.

8. Beaver Wars artifacts, "Historic Indian Artifacts," July 2004, Ohio Historical Society, July 2004, www.ohiohistory central.org.

9. David Van Tassel and John Grabowski, eds., "Immigration and Migration," *The Encyclopedia of Cleveland History* (Bloomington: Indiana Univ. Press, 1987), 557–63.

10. Ibid.

11. Ibid.

12. A sample can be seen in the John G. White Collection at the Cleveland Public Library, where many of Biehle's works on paper are stored.

13. Van Tassel and Grabowski, eds., "Industry," *Encyclopedia,* 566–68.

The Region's Man-Made Environment

1. Richard Fleischman, Creative Essence dialogue, Mar. 1, 2001, Shoreby Club.

2. See Robert C. Gaede and Robert Kalin, eds., *Guide to Cleveland Architecture* (Cleveland: AIA, 1991), 1, 3, 11, 25, 247, for information on the Burnham Plan, Erieview Plan, Historic Preservation, the inner ring suburbs, and the city's architectural firms.

3. Eric Johannesen, *Cleveland Architecture, 1876–1976* (Cleveland: Western Reserve Historical Society, 1979).

4. Peter Van Dijk, Creative Essence dialogue, Mar. 1, 2001, Shoreby Club.

5. Mary-Peale Schofield, *Landmark Architecture of Cleveland* (Pittsburgh: Ober Park Assoc., 1976).

6. *Slavic Village: Coming Home to the City* (Cleveland: Pulaski Franciscan Community Development Corp., 2002), 36–40; "Function, Form and Faith," videoconference series, Department of Education and Public Programs, Cleveland Museum of Art; Gaede and Kalin, eds., *Guide to Cleveland Architecture*, 151, 153–54.

7. Ted Sande, introduction to Gaede and Kalin, eds., *Guide to Cleveland Architecture.* Helpful resources on Cleveland architects in addition to Gaede and Kalin's *Guide to Cleveland Architecture* include Eric Johannesen's books *A Cleveland Legacy: The Architecture of Walker and Weeks* (Kent, Ohio: Kent State Univ. Press, 1999) and *Cleveland Architecture, 1876–1976,* as well as Schofield, *Landmark Architecture of Cleveland.*

8. Robert D. Kohn, "Architecture and Factories," *The Architectural Record* (Feb. 1909): 131–36; Schofield, *Landmark Architecture,* 115.

9. Johannesen, *Cleveland Architecture,* 198–99.

10. Karal Ann Marling, "New Deal Art in Cleveland," *Federal Art in Cleveland* (Cleveland: Cleveland Public Library, 1974), preface.

The Artists, Past and Present

1. "Artists, Past and Present," Creative Essence dialogue, Mar. 20, 2001, Cleveland Institute of Art.

2. William H. Robinson and David Steinberg, *Transformations in Cleveland Art,* exhibition catalog (Cleveland: Cleveland Museum of Art, 1996). See Selected Bibliography for several relevant publications.

3. William A. Millikin, *A Time Remembered* (Cleveland: Western Reserve Historical Society, 1975); Ruth Dancyger, "William Millikin," in *A Brush with Light: Watercolor Paint-*ers *of Northeast Ohio,* exhibition catalog (Cleveland: Cleveland Artists Foundation, 1998), 13–15.

4. William H. Robinson, *Clarence Carter: The Unknown Snapshot Studies, 1904–2000,* exhibition catalog (Portsmouth: Southern Ohio Museum, 2004), 33–34; Robert Sterns, ed., *Illusions of Eden: Visions of the American Heartland,* exhibition catalog (Columbus: Columbus Museum of Art/Arts Midwest/Ohio Arts Council, 2001), 254.

5. Quoted material from author's interviews with Lee-Smith at the Art Students' League, 1974, 1981, 1988; Romare Bearden and Harry Henderson, *A History of African-American Artists from 1792 to the Present* (New York: Pantheon, 1993), 328–36.

6. Mark Bassett and Victoria Naumann, *Cowan Pottery and the Cleveland School* (Atglen, Pa.: Schiffer, 1996), 45–49.

7. William Baran-Mickle, "Frederick A. Miller: A Precarious Balance," *Metalsmith* (Spring 1993): 34–38; Deborah Krupenia, "John Paul Miller," *American Craft Magazine* (Dec./Jan. 2003): 45–49; see also www.clevelandartsprize.org.

8. Ruth Dancyger, *Kubinyi and Hall,* Cleveland Artists Series (Cleveland: John Carroll University, 1998), 16, 24.

9. William H. Robinson, "Watercolor Painters of Northeast Ohio," in *A Brush with Light,* 27.

10. Christopher Finch, American Watercolors (New York: Abbeville Press, 1986).

11. Benjamin J. Townsend, "Crisis and Renewal: Charles Burchfield, 1915–16," in Nancy Weekly, *Life Cycles: The Charles Burchfield Collection* (Buffalo, N.Y.: The Burchfield-Penny Art Center, Buffalo State College, 1996), 96–122, esp. 100.

12. See Robinson and Steinberg, *Transformations in Cleveland's Art.*

13. Margaret Bourke-White, *Autobiography* (Boston: G. K. Hall, 1985); Vicki Goldberg, *Margaret Bourke-White* (New York: Harper and Row, 1986).

14. "Edris Eckhardt," Jay Hoffman, Jay, Dee Driscole, Mary Clare Zahler, *A Study in Regional Taste: The May Show 1919–1975,* exhibition catalog (Cleveland: Cleveland Museum of Art, 1977); Ruth Dancyger, *Edris Eckhardt, Cleveland Sculptor,* Cleveland Artists Series (Cleveland: John Carroll University, 1990).

15. Alfred L. Bright, "Cleveland Karamu Artists 1930–1945," paper and presentation, "Cleveland as a Center for Regional Art," Cleveland Artists Foundation, Nov. 1993.

16. *A Walking Tour and Guide to Cleveland Public Art* (Cleveland: Cleveland Public Art, 2003).

17. Henry Adams, *Paul Travis 1891–1975,* exhibition catalog (Cleveland: Cleveland Artists Foundation, 2001), 11–69; author discussion with art dealer of James Corcoran Fine Arts, Summer 2004.

18. Christine Fowler Shearer and William Robinson, *Carl Gaertner: A Story of Earth and Steel,* exhibition catalog (Cleveland: Cleveland Artists Foundation, 2000), 54; Robinson and Steinberg, "American Scene Movement in Cleveland," *Transformations in Cleveland Art,* 106–45.

19. Henry Adams, *Viktor Schreckengost and 20th Century Design,* exhibition catalog (Cleveland: Cleveland Museum of Art, 2000). See also www.viktorschreckengost.org.

20. "William McVey," Hoffman, Driscole, and Zahler, *A Study in Regional Taste,* 17

21. Note from student John Clague, July 7, 2004; www.clevelandartsprize.org, October 2002.

22. Sherman E. Lee's announcement for an exhibition of Joseph McCullough's paintings at the School of Fine Arts, in Willoughby, Ohio, 1975.

23. Joseph Kosuth, statement in artist's installation document for "Urban Evidence: Contemporary Artists Reveal Cleveland," the collaborative project of the Cleveland Center for Contemporary Art, the Cleveland Museum of Art, and SPACES, 1996; Elizabeth McClelland, "Edwin Mieczkowski, Neo-Constructivism," in Daniel H. Butts, Edward B Henning, Carolyn Jirousek, Elizabeth McClelland, *Harmonic Forms on the Edge: Geometric Abstraction in Cleveland,* exhibition catalog (Cleveland: Cleveland Artists Foundation, 2001); conversations with Ed Mieczkowski, esp. Feb. 2002–June 2004.

24. Jay Hoffman, Dee Driscole, Mary Clare Zahler, eds., *A Study in Regional Taste, The May Show 1919–1975,* exhibition catalog (Cleveland: CMA, 1977), 30–31.

25. Daniel H. Butts III, *Phyllis Sloane,* Ohio Artists Now monograph series (Cleveland: Cleveland Artists Foundation, 1996); see profile at www.clevelandartsprize.org.

26. Ruth Dancyger, *Phyllis Seltzer,* Ohio Artists Now monograph series (Cleveland: Cleveland Artists Foundation, 1996); see www.artistsarchives.org for profile and oral history.

27. See profile at www.clevelandartsprize.org, Fall 2002.

28. For full current biographical information on Cleveland Institute of Art faculty, see www.cia.edu; see also www.clevelandartsprize.org, Fall 2002.

29. On Kirk Mangus, *On Transcending Traditions: Ohio Artists in Clay and Fiber,* exhibition catalog (Columbus: Ohio Arts Council, 1999), 22–23; Tom Hinson, *The Invitational: Artists of Northeast Ohio,* exhibition catalog (Cleveland: CMA, 1991), 64.

30. Tom Hinson, *1994 Invitational: Artists of Northeast Ohio,* exhibition catalog (Cleveland: CMA, 1994), 56; Tom Hinson, *Urban Evidence: Artists Reveal Cleveland,* 2 vols. (Cleveland: CMA, 1996), 1:45, 2:42.

31. Henry Hawley, "Glass Today: American Studio Glass from Cleveland Collections," found at CMA website www.clevelandart.org.

32. "A City Seen: Photographs from the George Gund Foundation Collection," 2002, found at CMA website www.clevelandart.org; Kristin Chambers, *Dream Streets: The Urban Landscapes of Laurence Channing and Douglas Lucak. Exhibition* (Cleveland: Museum of Contemporary Art, 1999).

33. Conversation with Penny Rakoff, June 28, 2004.

34. Hinson, *The Invitational,* 17.

35. John Wood, "The Visionary Realism of Christopher Pekoc," *Strange Genius: The Journal of Contemporary Photography* 5 (2002); note from the artist, Aug. 12, 2004; Hinson, *The Invitational,* 38.

36. Roger Welchans, *David E. Davis: Transformations,* exhibition catalog (Youngstown, Ohio: Butler Institute of American Art, 2000); see also www.artistsarchives.org and www.sculpturecenter.org.

37. See www.sculpturecenter.org; conversation with the artist, Mar. 2003.

38. Elizabeth McClelland, *Cosmic Rays: The Public Sculpture of Athena Tacha,* exhibition catalog (Cleveland: Cleveland Artists Foundation, 1999); conversation with artist, Feb. 1999.

39. Tom Hinson, *Urban Evidence* 2:40.

40. Ibid., 12.

41. The exhibit was shown here at Lake Erie College in Apr. and May 1985. William Robinson, review of "From Provinces to Provincialism—20/20," *Dialogue* (July/Aug. 1985), reprinted in Elizabeth McClelland, *Cleveland Writers on Cleveland Artists: An Anthology,* Cleveland Artists Series (Cleveland: John Carroll University, 1990), 137.

42. Hinson, *1994 Invitational,* 9–11; Elizabeth McClelland, *Harmonic Forms on the Edge: Geometric Abstraction in Cleveland,* exhibition catalog (Cleveland: Cleveland Artists Foundation, 2001), 89; Elizabeth McClelland, "Julian Stanczak: Decades of Light," in *Cleveland Writers on Cleveland Artists,* 137; see also www.clevelandartsprize.org.

43. McClelland, *Harmonic Forms on the Edge,* 75–87; Edward Henning, essay for "Visual Logic" exhibition, cosponsored by the Cleveland Institute of Art and NOVA, 1979, reprinted in McClelland, *Cleveland Writers on Cleveland Artists,* 137.

44. Email from artist, Mar. 2003; conversation with artist, June 2003.

45. Elizabeth McClelland, review of "Rending Reality" exhibit, Mar. 1981, Cleveland State University, *Dialogue* (April/May 1981); note from William Busta, March 2003.

46. Hinson, *The Invitational*, 45–49, 32.

47. Ibid., 45–49.

48. Jay Hoffman, *A Study of Regional Taste*, exhibition catalog (Cleveland: Cleveland Museum of Art, 1977), 28–29; see also www.artistsarchives.org for an oral history, Aug. 9, 2004.

49. Elizabeth McClelland, *The Art of Mary Lou Ferbert,* Ohio Artists Now monograph series (Cleveland: Cleveland Artists Foundation, 1993); *Mary Lou Ferbert: Heroic Urban Wildflowers,* exhibition catalog (Cleveland: Bonfoey Company, 2002).

50. Conversations with the artist, esp. summer 2004; artist's oral history, at www.clevelandartsprize.org.

51. *Laurence Channing, Drawings 2000–2001,* exhibition catalog (Cleveland: Bonfoey Company, 2001). Kristin Chambers, "Dream Streets," Cleveland Center for Contemporary Art exhibition, May 1999, quoted in Ann Roulet, "About Artists (Cleveland: Cleveland Museum of Art/The Print Club of Cleveland, 2000).

52. See Ellen Landau's profile at www.clevelandartsprize.org.

53. Hinson, *The Invitational*, 13–17; Douglas Max Utter, *At the Edge of the Earth,* catalog for exhibition "Don Harvey: Invented Landscapes, a Ten Year Survey" (Cleveland: Cleveland Center for Contemporary Art, 2001).

54. Hinson, *The Invitational*, 26–27, and *Urban Evidence* 2:28–29.

55. Alfred L. Bright, Samuel W. Black, and Pamela McKee, *Yet Still We Rise: African American Art in Cleveland 1920–1970,* exhibition catalog (Cleveland: Cleveland Artists Foundation, 1996), 79.

56. Ibid., 56–57.

57. Notes from the artist, Mar. 2002.

58. Notes from the artist, Mar. 2003; conversation with the artist, June 2004.

59. *Yet Still We Rise,* 75–76; notes from Mona Phillips on Douglas Phillips, Aug. 2004.

Cleveland's Artistic Institutions

1. Margaret Lynch, "The Growth of Cleveland as a Cultural Center," in Thomas F. Campbell and Edward M. Miggins, eds., *The Birth of Modern Cleveland, 1865–1930* (Cleveland: Western Reserve Historical Society, 1988), 202.

2. Katharine Lee Reid, "Museums, Libraries and Other Collections," Creative Essence dialogue, Nov. 1, 2000, Cleveland Public Library.

3. Mitchell Kahan, "Contemporary Art, the Museum and Gallery" Creative Essence dialogue, Jan. 30, 2001, Cleveland Center for Contemporary Art.

4. Karel Ann Marling, *Federal Art in Cleveland, 1933–43* (Cleveland: CPL, 1974), vii.

5. Stephen Sietz, "Museums and Libraries" Creative Essence dialogue, November 1, 2000, Cleveland Public Library.

6. See *Art, Architecture, and the Collections of the Main Library: Public Art at the Cleveland Public Library* (Cleveland: Cleveland Public Library, 1999).

7. Nancy Coe Wixom, *Cleveland Institute of Art: The First Hundred Years, 1882–1982* (Cleveland: Cleveland Institute of Art, 1983), 13. See also www.cia.edu.

8. Discussions with artist, esp. May 2002–Feb. 2003.

9. Correspondence with Jane Tesso, curator of art, BP America, summer 2000.

Forging the Future

1. John Villani, *The 100 Best Small Art Towns in America,* 3d ed. (Santa Fe, N.M.: John Muir Publications, 1998).

2. See the Partnership website at www.cultureplan.org.

3. Robert Gaede, "Historic Restoration, Historic Preservation, Adaptive Reuse and Exceptional Maintenance," document prepared for Cleveland Artists Foundation, July 2000.

4. Steven Litt's canal series, *Plain Dealer,* Nov. 2000. *Plain Dealer* art and architecture critic Steven Litt has written and spoken eloquently on these subjects in speeches, on panels, and in articles.

5. William Busta, "Contemporary Art, the Museum and Gallery," Creative Essence dialogue, Jan. 30, 2001, Cleveland Center for Contemporary Art.

6. Correspondence and discussion with Foster Armstrong, Jan.–Feb. 2000.

Appendix A: An Annotated List of Artists and Images

George C. Adomeit (1879–1967): *Farm Landscape–Ohio,* 1899, oil on canvas, 9" x 12" (photograph by William Pinter); *Chagrin Valley,* ca. 1940, oil on canvas board, 16" x 20" (photograph by William Pinter), the Shoreby Club.

Between 1899 and 1940 Adromeit was president and art director of the Caxton Company, a printing and engraving company. His paintings and drawings were exhibited at forty consecutive May Shows, where he won twenty-four awards. His American scene paintings follow him from Zoar and Berlin Heights to his summer trips on the East Coast and in Mexico, Canada, and Brazil. His style, soft and painterly early, later shows influence of the harder edge of the work he did as a printer and engraver.

Kenneth Bates (1904–1994): *Oriental Casket,* 1966, cloisonné, 2" x 1½" x 3", Elaine and Joseph Kisvardai.

Bates was an excellent colorist, designer, and craftsman who explored the endless possibilities of enameling and experimented with translating two-dimensional design into three dimensions. To gain different effects, he would use a welding torch on copper sheets to create a surface with holes or rippled edges and incorporate different materials and found objects with enamel to produce wonderful textures. This work is perhaps an example of shapes in his own garden; he took inspiration for his work from nature. His work won many prizes at the May Shows. Head of the Design Department of the Cleveland School of Art, he wrote on both design and enameling techniques. His book, *The Enamelist,* has been a main resource since its publication.

August Biehle (1885–1979): *View of Canal,* ca. 1940, oil on canvas, 31½" x 38¼" (photograph by Berni Rich), the Janet

Alder Family; *Overgrown Hermitage Along Road to Zoar,* ca. 1920, gouache and pencil, 18' x 24" (photograph by Berni Rich), Janet Alder family; *Berlin Heights Farmhouse,* ca. 1920s, oil on canvas, 26" x 34", Hahn Loeser & Parks LLP; *Tug on the Cuyahoga,* 1932, lithograph, 8" x 12", Cleveland Artists Foundation, gift of Frederick and Helen Biehle; Kokoon Club poster, 1937, lithograph, 21" x 13", Elaine and Joseph Kisvardai.

Thanks to diligent recording that includes a complete video and documented distribution of August Biehle's work, Biehle's interest in scene painting in a variety of styles is preserved. He worked in the commercial world of the Sherwin-Williams Paint Company and lithography. Biehle joined with the Berlin Heights artists, and his work was shown in many group shows in the galleries through the 1970s.

Margaret Bourke-White (1904–1971): *Blast Furnace Operator with "Mud Gun" Otis Steel Company,* ca. 1928, gelatin silver print, 13" x 10¼", the Cleveland Museum of Art, gift of Mrs. Albert A. Levin; reprinted with permission of the Estate of Margaret Bourke-White.

This artist started her career in Cleveland, and her camera recorded the spirit of this working city by focusing on the steel industry. She moved away from Cleveland when her work attracted national notice and assignments for *Fortune* and *Life* magazines. Bourke-White captured both the beauty and awkwardness of industry. Her influence here can be seen best in the paintings of Carl Gaertner. Both are masters of the fusion of light and dark in the environments of industry.

Elmer Brown (1909–1977): *Freedom of Speech,* 1942 (restored 1990), oil on masonite, 8'10" x 21', City Club of Cleveland.

This social realist painter was commissioned through the WPA by the City Club to create this work to represent its essence of justice, freedom, honor, and the free exchange of ideas. Looking carefully, one finds "icons" representing these ideals: the Magna Carta, the Bill of Rights, the Declaration of Independence, the U.S. Constitution, the Scales of Justice. Brown studied at the Cleveland Institute of Art and taught at Karamu House. He illustrated some of his friend Langston Hughes's books and then worked for American Greetings Corporation for the last eighteen years of his career.

Malcolm Brown (b. 1931): *Jazz Messengers,* 1998, ceramic tile, 8' x 6', Langston Hughes Branch, Cleveland Public Library, courtesy of the Malcolm Brown Gallery.

A nationally recognized watercolorist, Brown has been working and teaching in the Cleveland area throughout his career. Working in soft colors with a loose stroke, Brown's work is at times abstract and at other moments evocative of scenes of city life. He has had several solo exhibitions in Ohio and other states including West Virginia, Kansas, Georgia, and North Carolina. His public commissions have occurred nationally. Brown has been a member of the American Watercolor Society since 1973 and a charter member of the Ohio Watercolor Society.

Charles Burchfield (1893–1967): *Retreat of Winter,* 1937, watercolor, 11" x 17" (photograph by William Pinter), Jay and Kathy Ferrari.

Burchfield studied at the Cleveland School of Art with Frederick Gottwald, Henry Keller, and Frank Wilcox, and later he joined William Sommer at Brandywine and the Berlin Heights artists near Sandusky. Over the first quarter of the century, he had two solo exhibitions at the Cleveland School of Art and exhibited at venues like the Cleveland Play House, Laukhuff's Bookstore, the May Show of the Cleveland Museum of Art, and other venues. After 1921 he moved to Buffalo where he first became a wallpaper designer and then a full-time painter. His solo shows were held at New York's Museum of Modern Art, the Pittsburgh Carnegie Institute of Art, and Buffalo's Albright-Knox Galleries. The Whitney Museum of American Art organized a major exhibition of his work that traveled to the Cleveland Museum of Art. Because of that exhibit, *Time* magazine called him the "best US watercolorist." He was eulogized by President Lyndon Johnson as an "artist to America" on his death in 1967. Burchfield always gave homage to his Cleveland beginnings and teachers, most notably Henry Keller.

Shirley Aley Campbell (b. 1925): *Per Carnum,* 2004, oil, 30" x 40".

Draftsmanship is at the core of Shirley Aley Campbell's every work, and her skill is honed to a level of strength that is rare. Since the beginning of her career in the 1940s, her style has changed from figurative expressionism to total abstraction, and since the 1970s, from hard-edged realism toward a freer, more painterly realism, sometimes incorporating collage elements. She was three-time first prize–winner in painting in the Cleveland Museum of Art's May Show, was included in the retrospective exhibit of 1977, and was awarded the Cleveland Fine Arts Prize Award in 1986. Her work is included in the collections of most of the museums in northeast Ohio as well as the museums of art in Evanston, Illinois, and Kansas City, Missouri, and at UCLA.

Clarence Carter (1904–2000): *William Millikin on His Way to the Century of Progress Exposition,* 1933, oil on canvas, 29⅛" x 43⅛", Cleveland Museum of Art, Mr. and Mrs. William H. Marlatt Fund.

Carter taught at the CMA in the 1930s and served as Millikin's northeast Ohio district supervisor of the Federal Arts Project. He described Millikin mentor as a "towering personality in the world of art," and photographs and this painting are testimony and memorial to his friend. Carter's best-known paintings record specific regional subjects. On his ninetieth birthday in 1994, Carter was given a retrospective exhibition at the Southern Ohio Museum in Portsmouth. His work is included in the permanent collections of the Brooklyn Museum of Art, the Butler Institute of American Art, the Nelson-Atkins Museum of Art, and the Whitney Museum of American Art. He was awarded a Cleveland Arts Prize in 1972.

H. C. Cassill (b. 1928): *Icarus,* 1958, intaglio, 27¾" x 20½".

This print won a special award at the 1958 May Show. Cassill's prints have always been provocative and multilayered in content and context. This work was seen as using the Icarus story as metaphor for the falling human figure and its resurrection in art. From 1957 he headed the Printmaking Department at the Cleveland Institute of Art. In 1971 he became the first printmaker to win the Visual Arts Award of the Women's City Club.

Laurence Channing (b. 1942): *North Light,* 2001, image, 4½" x 4½", paper 14" x 15", charcoal on Reeves BFK, Diane Schaffstein.

Channing's subject is the city street. In working with photographs, he abstracts the elements to create a composition reminding us of scenes that we know, forms that intrigue, and perspectives that are fresh. His work is in many important collections including the Cleveland Museum of Art, Progressive Insurance Company, and the Federal Reserve Bank. He has been honored by two Ohio Arts Council individual artist fellowships, many solo exhibits at the Bonfoey Company, and the Cleveland Arts Prize in 2000.

John Clague (1928–2004): *Progression in Black and White,* 1963, black-and-white painted steel, 68', Cleveland Museum of Art, the Wishing Well Fund.

John Clague is inspired by organic forms. The work shown explores nonrepresentational planes, shapes defined by color, and patterns that change as one walks around it. Clague also explores kinetic sculptures that are sound producing and two-dimensional polished steel surfaces. He exhibited many works in the May Show. In 1967 he was awarded the Cleveland Arts Prize in 1967. His work has been included in many museum exhibits including the Whitney Museum of American Art, New York City.

Allen E. Cole (1883–1970): *Call and Post Newsboys,* undated, photograph, Western Reserve Historical Society.

A popular photographer, Cole's work documents midtwentieth century African American life, history, and culture from 1919 until his retirement in 1969. The Western Reserve Historical Society acquired the collection in 1979 that includes nearly 30,000 negatives, 6,000 original prints, four 16mm films, and an oil painting.

Johnny Coleman (b. 1958): *Northern Ohio Crossroads,* 1996, mixed media installation, "Urban Evidence: Contemporary Artists Reveal Cleveland," SPACES.

The raw and found materials incorporated in this piece tell a lot about Johnny Coleman's concerns and work. In this piece he sought to unearth the stories of the African Americans that came north with the migrations and inhabited the neighborhoods, using interviews he conducted with several generations of black Clevelanders.

Willard Combes (1901–1984): *Annual Exhibition of Cleveland Artists and Craftsmen of the Western Reserve, or The May Show,* ca. 1940, ink on illustration board, 16½" x 13¾", the Cleveland Artists Foundation, gift of Jean Combes.

Willard Combes, an editorial cartoonist for the *Cleveland Press,* was perhaps best known for his World War II cartoons that focused on the sale of War Bonds. He was also a portrait artist, muralist, and stained-glass maker.

Claude Conover (1907–1993): *Chab,* 1961, stoneware, 19" x 16", Elaine and Joseph Kisvardai.

Claude Conover worked for thirty years as a commercial designer before turning to ceramics. By the 1960s he was devoting himself full time to his pots. He exhibited in fourteen May Shows, and his work was shown in forty-seven exhibitions at museums and arts centers around the country, some traveling internationally. Many regional patrons have made these hand-built stoneware pots part of their home environment.

Cowan Pottery Studios (1913–1931): *Flower Frog Figurines,* 1925–31, Cowan Pottery Collection, Cowan Pottery Museum, Rocky River Public Library.

The Cowan Pottery Studios, under the artistic leadership of ceramicist R. Guy Cowan (1884–1957), was a laboratory for experimentation with glazes, forms, and the marketing of art craft.

David Davis (1920–2002): *David Berger National Memorial Monument,* 1974, corten steel, 14' x 11' x 11', Mayfield Jewish Community Center, Cleveland Heights, Ohio.

David Davis's sculpture is a memorial to David Berger, a Clevelander who lived in Israel and who was one of the eleven athletes killed at the Olympic Games in Munich in 1972. The piece was designated a National Memorial by the National Park Service in 1980. Davis's work is in many visible locations in this region—in front of the original Progressive Insurance Building, the Beck Center for the Arts, the Free Clinic, the Beachwood Library. He founded the Sculpture Center and the Artists Archives of the Western Reserve.

Clara Deike (1881–1964): *The Willow,* 1910, oil, 16" x 20", Richard A. Zellner.

Deike, who taught in the Cleveland Public Schools between 1912 and 1945, studied with well-known mentor-teachers such as Hans Hofmann in Italy and Diego Rivera in Mexico. During the time with Rivera her work changed profoundly to reflect the influence of his cubist perspective. She was noted early for her decorative landscapes, especially for her feeling for trees and her ability to paint them.

Edris Eckhardt (1907–1998): *The Three Ages of Man,* 1956, gold glass, 7¼" x 4", Elaine and Joseph Kisvardai.

Working in both ceramics and glass, Eckhardt is remembered in the art world for rediscovering an Egyptian art of fusing gold leaf between sheets of glass to produce gold glass. Her subjects ranged from those out of storybooks to the complex theme of this piece. She taught ceramics at the Cleveland School of Art, was this region's Supervisor for Sculpture for the Federal Arts Project, and received two Guggenheim Fellowships.

Mary Lou Ferbert (b. 1924): *Old Door,* 1993, transparent watercolor, 85" x 41½".

Mary Lou Ferbert combines natural and man-made images, uniting them from a unique perspective, simplifying and abstracting them. The result is the expansion of the potential of watercolor to high-energy painting. In the 1980s she began to focus on wildflowers that adapt and survive in an often hostile, biologically sterile cityscape. Recently she has embarked on a new series of large paintings that present these pioneering wildflowers in a scale commensurate with their strength, survival capacities, and beauty. She has had solo exhibitions at the Bonfoey Company, the Butler Institute of American Art, and Gallery Madison 90, New York City, among others. Among the collections that include her work are the Cleveland Museum of Natural History, El Paso (Texas) Museum of Art, and the National Museum of Women in the Arts, Rutgers University.

Richard Fleischman and Partners, Architects, Inc.: Ohio Aerospace Institute, 1993.

During forty years of conceptualizing various projects, Richard Fleischman (b. 1928) has led this firm with a unique sense of modernism—one in which there is a fusion of innovation and available technology. The 400 projects designed by this firm over the last decades are the cutting edge in Cleveland architecture. The firm's buildings have won international awards, and its architects have designed projects for cultural institutions, educational facilities, and corporation headquarters. The firm was awarded the American Institute of Architects Ohio Gold Medal Firm Award in 1988 and received the Cleveland Prize and Fleischman's Arts in Architecture Award in 1974.

Carl Floyd (b. 1936): *Tempus Pons,* 1984–85, sculpture, stone and concrete and ceramic tiles, City of Cleveland, (photograph by William Pinter).

Since 1967 Carl Floyd has focused on developing large-scale site-specific sculptures. This piece, which was selected from nine designs through a competition sponsored by the Ohio Arts Council for the development of a work in the Market Square (across from the West Side Market), is made up of about 1,000 ceramic tiles made by residents of the West Side neighborhoods. Some of his other site-specific projects can be seen in Marietta, Perry, and Vermillion, Ohio.

Carl Gaertner (1898–1952): *Bend on the Storm King,* gouache and oil, 24" x 39" (photograph by Rob Muller), Frances and Seth Taft; *Steel Mills on the Cuyahoga,* ca. 1928, oil on canvas, 24½" x 28¾", Hahn Loeser & Parks LLP.

A nationally recognized artist of American scene subjects, Gaertner traveled throughout Ohio and went on summer painting excursions to Provincetown, Massachusetts, with George Adomeit and others. His work was shown at the Cleveland Museum of Art from 1922 to 1953, and widely elsewhere. He taught at the Cleveland Institute of Art from 1925 to 1952. *Steel Mills* is one of the special examples of Gaertner's ability to abstract both atmosphere and industrial shape. He has captured the essence and drama of the industrial night scene.

Frederick C. Gottwald (1858–1941): *Cleveland Market,* ca. 1895, oil on canvas, 13⅛" x 18¼", Federal Reserve Bank, Cleveland.

Gottwald's influence on the early art scene cannot be overestimated. Gottwald studied in Munich before settling in Cleveland. His style was influenced by his traditional Germanic studies and the new impressionism he saw in the art world and in the homes of art-collecting Clevelanders. Not always in sympathy with the new style of painting, he acknowledged its influence. Gottwald taught at the Cleveland School of Art from 1885 until 1926 and instructed future artists like Keller, Wilcox, and Travis. His work was regularly displayed at the National Academy of Design.

Henry Halem (b. 1938): *Roman Display Vessel,* 2001, glass and aluminum, 21" x 17" x 6".

Henry Halem has exhibited extensively since 1969. He taught glass work at Kent State University for twenty-nine years and received the President's Medal for Outstanding Achievement because of his work there. He also received the 1994 Governor's Award from the State of Ohio. His glass work has been included in international exhibits and is in the permanent collections of many museums, including the Corning Museum of Glass, the Smithsonian Institution, and the Cleveland Museum of Art. Public art commissions include a large cast glass wall executed with Brinsley Tyrrell for RTA.

Don Harvey (b. 1941): *Bad Water,* 1991, photograph on aluminum, steel, and rubber, 74" x 84" x 3", Cleveland Museum of Art, gift of Mr. and Mrs. Richard A. Zellner.

Harvey's influences are the industrial environment and the lake, and his use of steel and rubber reflect the materials of the region's history. His work has been exhibited in all of the major venues in the city. He spearheaded the development of Cleveland Public Art, was awarded the Cleveland Fine Arts Prize in Visual Arts in 1991, and was the original managing editor of *Dialogue Magazine*.

Masumi Hayashi (b. 1945): *Cleveland Cultural Gardens*, 1987, panoramic photo collage, 39' x 61", Kodak paper, artist's proof; *Public Square, Cleveland, Ohio*, 1994, panoramic photo collage, 20" x 56".

Masumi Hayashi constructs a panoramic view by joining small photographs together. This technique produces a visual energy around the setting. Her work, which has been especially thought provoking for its multivisual layering, is internationally recognized with exhibition and awards as her horizon expands.

Hope Memorial Bridge (1932), Lorain-Carnegie Pylons, architect Frank Walker (1877–1949), sculptor Henry Hering (1876–1949).

Giant art deco figures serve as gateways to Cleveland's East and West Sides. Hermes, holding a tank truck in one hand and a coal hauler in the other, symbolizes the progress of transportation. The forty-three foot pylons are made of local Berea sandstone. This is one of the many bridges over the Cuyahoga that stand as symbols of this working city and demonstrate the beauty of industrial form.

Mark Howard (b. 1963): *Third Precinct*, 1996, laser-cut mirrored Plexiglas on painted wood panel, 76" x 75", Hahn Loeser & Parks LLP.

Mark Howard is an observer of the city neighborhood, drawing inspiration from it and creating recognizable yet mysterious and powerful works. The text for *Third Precinct*, which was found in a police station, was translated into laser cutouts. This relief sculpture was originally part of the "Urban Evidence: Contemporary Artists Reveal Cleveland" installation at the Cleveland Center for Contemporary Art (now Museum of Modern Art Cleveland). Mark Howard has had other major commissions, including the ceiling *Clio and the Death of Hyacinthus* on the sixth floor of the Louis Stokes wing at the Cleveland Public Library.

Max Kalish (1891–1945): *Abraham Lincoln*, 1928–32, bronze statue, permission from Don Kalish and the Sculpture Center.

Max Kalish studied sculpture as a teenager under Herman Matsen at the Cleveland School of Art and went to New York and Europe for more study. For many years the themes of his bronze sculptures were of laborers. The Lincoln statue may be his only work displayed out of doors.

He exhibited his work in Philadelphia, New York, and Chicago as well as in Cleveland.

Gene Kangas (b. 1944): *Hart Crane Memorial*, 1995, painted steel and corten, Ohio Canal Corridor.

This memorial is the last sculpture piece to be supported by the Mildred Andrews Fund that supported many of the works in the University Circle area. The Hart Crane Memorial Park is at Columbus Road as it crosses under the Detroit-Superior Bridge. Other Kangas work is located in the corner of the State Office building, at the Justice Center, and on the Case Western Reserve University campus. He was professor of Sculpture at Cleveland State University from 1971 to 1998.

Henry Keller (1869–1949): *The William Lee Farm, Berlin Heights*, 1915, oil on board, 20" x 14", Cleveland Artists Foundation, gift of Karl Humm; *View of Cleveland*, ca. 1930, watercolor on paper, 18¾" x 12¾", Cleveland Artists Foundation, gift of Dorothy Beck.

Henry Keller encouraged the modernist movement in Cleveland and was known for his watercolors. The consummate teacher and mentor invited his peers and students to join him in Berlin Heights at his family-owned farm and there encouraged them to explore the countryside, beaches, and environment around them. He exhibited at the New York Armory Show, a pivotal moment in the annals of art history for its presentation of European art and its influence on American art. He also exhibited at the May Show of the Cleveland Museum of Art, the Carnegie International Shows in Pittsburgh, the annual shows at the Academy of Fine Arts in Philadelphia, and at the Whitney Museum of American Art.

Kalman Kubinyi (1906–1973): *Railroad Crossing*, ca. 1935–39, lithograph, 14" x 9¾", WPA Prints, Special Collections, Case Western Reserve University.

Kubinyi was active as an artist, teacher, and administrator. A deeply committed community coordinator, he founded and headed the Cleveland Printmakers and the Cleveland Print Market. Between 1935 and 1939 he supervised the Graphics Arts Project of the WPA and then the entire district WPA project. The subjects of many WPA prints were of workers or work scenes with clear social entendre. Kubinyi exhibited in print shows in many cities in the United States and as far away as New York and Venice.

Hughie Lee-Smith (1915–2000): *Counterpoise II*, 1989, oil on canvas, 26" x 32", Charles and Frances Debordeau.

Hughie Lee-Smith was influenced by his teachers Henry Keller and Carl Gaertner, who showed him the importance of values, which was always reflected in his work. Fifty years after he started painting and after winning many recognitions, there was a major retrospective of his work with reviews in major publications in 1988. He had had more than forty solo exhibitions from 1945 until the 1990s. He is thought to be the most highly acclaimed African American artist to have started his career in Cleveland.

Michael Loderstedt (b. 1958): *Fairplay,* 1996, "Urban Evidence: Contemporary Artists Reveal Cleveland," Cleveland Museum of Art.

Wrapping three walls of a gallery in the Cleveland Museum of Art with a black-and-white panorama of the harbor and shore photographed from the water, Loderstedt's *Fairplay* lets us see the city as many land dwellers never do. In the center of the gallery, a full-size sailboat lists to one side on the floor/water, suggesting both the exhilarating freedom of the open water and the vessel's function as haven from hostile elements. Loderstedt's work, which usually combines more than one medium, has been included in two seminal exhibits at the Cleveland Museum of Art: the 1996 invitational exhibit "Urban Evidence" and the 1999 "Cleveland Collects" exhibit. He has taught at Kent State University since 1988 and is a 1999 recipient of an Ohio Arts Council Artists Fellowship Award.

Michelangelo Lovelace (b. 1960): *Born Again,* 2000, mural at 36th Street and Cedar Avenue.

Lovelace's murals are reflections on the life of urban African Americans in the United States today and involve themes of cultural, racial, and economic tensions in the inner city. Lovelace's interest and focus on developing his painting career stems from persistence, mentoring, self-confidence, and skills—and his genial yet tough personality.

Douglas Lucak (b. 1959): *Radiance and Industry,* 1995, black-and-white photograph, oil paint, 2¾" x 7⅛".

Working with pinhole photography because of its simplicity and depth of field, Lucak gives us incredible views of the city—its streets, alleys, paths, highways, houses, and buildings. The imprecise pinhole introduces an element of chance; and after he tones the images to effect a fuzzy ethereal image, the result is a work filled with feeling. Lucak sets his cameras on stoops or between guardrails or wherever to record his unforgettable images. He has had numerous solo exhibits and been included in many group exhibits. His work is included in the collections of the Pro-

gressive Corporation, the George Gund Foundation, the Cleveland Museum of Art, and, in London, the LeBoeuf, Lamb, Greene and MacCrae collection. He was awarded an Ohio Arts Council Individual Fellowship in 2003.

Craig Lucas (b. 1941): *Echo,* 1994, oil, wax, and flashe, 80" x 66", Progressive Corporation.

Lucas's paintings of this period are imposing abstract compositions that striate layers of paint on top of shapes beneath, making for a fascinating fusion of color and form. Lucas was a student and has been a professor at Kent State University. His work has been exhibited in many cities in Ohio and in Toronto, Los Angeles, and New York City.

Clarence Mack (1888–1982): Lakewood house, architectural design (photograph by Al Teufen).

For the thirty-two houses he designed in northern Ohio between 1914 and 1938, Clarence Mack adapted established traditional exterior styles to the needs of his clients. He used classic proportions, symmetry, and doorways that brought the details of French eclectic style and Georgian architecture to these buildings. The interiors were equally carefully designed, elegant, and polished.

Kirk Mangus (b. 1952): *Big Bug Jar,* 1989, wood-fired stoneware, 29" x 15" diameter, British Petroleum.

Mangus's works have been described as borrowing the sensibility of early Asian ceramics and classic Greek vases. *Big Bug Jar* is a basic jar form with carvings deep enough to perforate the vessel wall in several places and rhythmically grouped calligraphic lines. His ceramic pieces have been shown in solo and group exhibits in this region and throughout the United States, including the Seattle Art Museum and the Renwick Gallery in Washington, D.C.

Jim Mazurkewicz (b. 1943): *Comet of the Millenium,* 2000, 18K yellow gold, 1 ct. total weight of diamonds, and Tahitian black pearl, 2" x 1" x ½".

Mazurkewicz, who studied with both Frederick Miller and John Paul Miller, designs unique, sought-after jewelry as Designer-Goldsmith for Potter and Mellen, Inc., keeping alive a long and internationally respected craft tradition in Cleveland.

Joseph McCullough (b. 1923): *Red Sounds,* 1967, acrylic, 40" x 50", Betty and Osman K. Mawardi.

McCullough, who came to the scene in the 1950s to teach and then to head the Cleveland Institute of Art, replaced theories of color that had been taught there for many years.

His training was grounded at the school with Rolf Stoll, William Eastman, and Paul Travis, and his work with Josef Albers at Yale solidified the groundwork for his innovative "Color and Light" course. McCullough was a civic presence as head of the Fine Arts Advisory Committee of Cleveland's City Planning Commission for twenty years. The Institute's extension, the renovated old Ford Factory building near the main building, is named the McCullough Center for the Visual Arts. McCullough won the Cleveland Arts Prize for the Visual Arts in 1970.

Leza McVey (1907–1984): *Detail of Rug*, colored squares of woolen material, 9' x 9' (photograph by Rob Muller), Frances and Seth Taft.

Without predesigning, McVey spent three years creating this original design using a traditional weaving method. Her colors are a rich mix of muted tones like avocado green, purple, and lavenders; her patterns are squares and diagonals that evolved as she created. McVey's early career as a ceramist was documented in a book titled *The Ceramic Forms of Leza McVey* (2003). Her eye conditions, Malta fever and glaucoma, caused her to move to textile design and production.

William McVey (1905–1999): *Tom Johnson*, 1987, bronze sculpture on granite base (photograph by the Sculpture Center), Case Western Reserve University at the Western Reserve Historical Society.

McVey's reputation was made after he received in 1963 the commission from the British government for a statue of Winston Churchill to be placed at the Washington, D.C., embassy. In this region we recognize his wide-ranging concepts and styles in the relief of Paul Bunyan at the Lakeview Terrace and statues of Tom Johnson in the courtyard of the Western Reserve Historical Society and Hart Crane on the campus of Case Western Reserve University.

Edwin Mieczkowski (b. 1929): *Sommer's Sun*, 1978, oil on canvas, tondo (photograph by Peter Hastings), Cleveland Public Library; *Blue and White Ford*, 1966, acrylic on canvas, 47" x 41.5", Cleveland Museum of Art, Wishing Well Fund.

Mieczkowski has been a force on the Cleveland arts scene for over fifty years as a teacher and painter. His paintings are structural and layered and, because of the force of dynamic color, are in relief even when they are sculptural. His *Sommer's Sun* mural is a tondo that is placed at a right angle to the William Sommer mural, *The City in 1833*, at the Cleveland Public Library, Brett Hall. It takes its theme and colors from the Sommer mural and has been described

as the epitome of radiant sun. His public work include an eleven-color geometric abstract mural on the Halle Building that was replaced by the Windham Hotel.

Frederick Miller (1913–2000): *Pitcher*, 1961, sterling silver and ebony, 11½", Smithsonian Institution.

A student of Horace Potter, Miller established the jewelry design and silversmith program at the Cleveland School of Art as well as at the Potter and Mellen store, which he eventually bought, carrying on the legacy that still exists today. His silver craft was art—usable and beautiful, modern and traditional. He loved his material and sought to work in new free forms, especially bowls, which expanded the rules of design and application in hollow ware. He received many major awards and made twenty-one consecutive appearances in the May Show. He garnered national attention and acclaim through exhibitions, awards, articles, and films. At one time, every major silver company in North America had employed a former student of his. He received the Cleveland Arts Prize in 1968.

John Paul Miller (b. 1918): *Cephalopod*, 1978, 18K gold and pure gold with enamel, 3⅛" x 1⅜".

Miller's rediscovery of granulation, the ancient Etruscan technique of fusing metal without the use of solder, has been at the core of his invention and acclaim. He is perhaps best known for his unique renditions of sea creatures. Miller's work has been included in many solo exhibitions, including the Art Institute of Chicago, and in many group exhibitions in this country and abroad, including the Vatican Museum in Italy and the Victoria and Albert Museum in London. Miller received the 1994 American Craft Council gold medal award for artistic excellence and the Cleveland Arts Prize in 1968.

John Moore (1940): *Bill*, 1989, oil on canvas, 66" x 78", Hahn Loeser & Parks LLP.

This painting's smooth dark oval shapes, almost human in form, seem as if they are moving across the space, resembling a rough sea of contrasting, uneven, aggressive brush strokes. John Moore was born in Cleveland and worked at General Motors before he focused on his education. He received his BFA and MFA from Kent State University and taught at Cuyahoga Community College and in the Art History and Education Department of the Cleveland Museum of Art, of which he was also assistant curator. He has received artist fellowships from the Ohio Arts Council, the National Endowment for the Arts, and the New York Foundation for the Arts. His work has been featured in more than eighteen solo exhibitions, including at the Akron Art Museum, the High Museum of Art in Atlanta, and the Cleveland Center for Contemporary Art.

Holly Morrison (b. 1959): *Facing North,* 1995–96, 4 gelatin silver print photographs, each 40" x 40", Federal Reserve Bank of Cleveland; *The Golden Game,* 1997, painted ceiling and walls (photograph by Don Snyder), Cleveland Public Library.

Coming from the flat lands and sand hills of Nebraska to the banks of the Cuyahoga River and Lake Erie, Morrison accepted a faculty position at the Cleveland Institute of Art in the early 1990s. Holly has been drawn to the city and its images. *Facing North* chronicles the serenity of a year in the life of Lake Erie. A set of eight photographs out of 300 are now in collection of the Federal Reserve Bank. Four from the set of eight pictures depict the changing values of the sky and lake during the four seasons. *The Golden Game* mural can be seen at the northwest corner tower of the fifth floor of the Cleveland Public Library's Main Branch. Painted directly on the ceiling and walls in blue, silver, and gold, the mural gives the ceiling a vaulted look. The figurative gold images and silver glyphs are taken from books on alchemy. The ceiling works as a transition space between earth and sky.

Ken Nevadomi (b. 1939): *Man Who Lived in a Refrigerator,* 1985, acrylic, 66" x 66".

Nevadomi's paintings attract attention for their intriguing subject matter and haunting mystery. Human figures are usually painted flat and stylized, acting as conveyors of basic shapes, gestures, expressions, and movement. Emanating from a vast array of interests and experiences, his painterly style incorporates aggressive subject matter simmering with provocation. Nevadomi has been exhibiting in solo and group exhibitions mostly in Ohio. The traveling exhibition "The 39th Biennial Exhibition of Contemporary American Painting," included his work.

Nottingham-Spirk Design Associates: Little Tikes Kitchen, 1977–90, rotational molded plastic, 17" x 15" x 36".

Nottingham-Spirk has been a major design force here and nationally. Products of the Cleveland Institute of Art, John Nottingham and John Spirk grew a firm that has become one of the leading new product invention and development groups in the country. Local companies like Little Tikes, Royal/Dirt Devil, Manco, and Sherwin-Williams have used Nottingham-Spirk designs.

Old Arcade: (1890) This landmark was inspired by European atrium arcades in Milan and England, as well as by the work of Henry Hobson Richardson (1838–85), one of America's most prominent late-nineteenth-century architects. The Euclid and Superior Street facades, with their massive stone Romanesque forms, include windows lined up under multistoried arcades. The interior, still dominated by its monumental staircase, is resplendent with restored brass and woodwork and a new glass atrium. This building, the place for past Easter parades and political conventions, now houses the Hyatt Regency Hotel.

Joseph O'Sickey (b. 1918): *In the Garden,* 1972, oil, 62" x 48", Frances and Seth Taft.

Joseph O'Sickey's popular work ties us to the color and joy of the indoor and outdoor scenes we know from the impressionists and post-impressionists. His paintings are about places we know; they are reminiscent of many things recognizable and part of our own experiences. O'Sickey's life as an artist began very early and developed as teachers in elementary school, East Technical High School, and the Cleveland School of Art recognized his talent. In the late 1930s he studied with Henry Keller, William Eastman, Carl Gaertner, Frank Wilcox, Kenneth Bates, and Viktor Schreckengost at the school and with Rolf Stoll and Paul Travis at Huntington Polytechnic. O'Sickey was an instructor at the Akron Art Institute and Case Western Reserve University, and he helped develop Kent State University's Blossom Summer Arts Program in the late 1960s. His list of "first" painting awards and prizes is long and culminated with the Cleveland Arts prize in 1974.

Patricia Zinsmeister Parker (b. 1934): *Cuffs-links,* 1990, diptych, latex enamel, oil, and cardboard on canvas, 74" x 136", Hahn Loeser & Parks LLP.

Parker's abstract idiom is influenced by patterns she has seen in ceramic work and textiles. This work is a diptych, but Parker painted each piece separately and then placed them side by side, one on top of the other, turning them horizontally and vertically until she found the coherent whole. Many of Parker's works have richly built-up surfaces and collage elements and incorporate words or statements.

John Pearson (b. 1940): *Mondrian Linear Series,* 1977, silkscreen inks on acrylic over canvas, 210" x 660' x 4", Cleveland Justice Center.

Pearson is a systemic artist, carefully organizing his work around sequences of shape, color, and line, beginning with an idea that has multiple possibilities for satisfying resolutions. In the *Mondrian Series* (titled because of his Mondrian-like palette of red, yellow, blue, black, white, and gray) the artist moved the silkscreen over the surface of the canvas until the painting was completed as a rich complex pattern of angled lines on the multicolored background. The color sequences and movement of the lines draw the viewer into the web of the work. His most recent work evolves beyond strict geometry (especially grids) to harmonic forms synthesizing his experience and reflection. Pearson comes from a background of teaching, traveling, and exhibiting in many areas of the world. He is the Young-Hunter Professor of Studio Art at Oberlin College, where he has taught for thirty years.

Christopher Pekoc (b. 1941): *Ritual of Inquiry,* 1997–98, mixed media on electrostatic prints, paper, and polyester film with machine stitching, 26½" x 103", Case Western Reserve University, Baer and Hiltner Collection.

Pekoc's work has come full circle—from using the photographs to make his work to making the photographs the real works of art. His work has gained internal recognition and is presently included in the prestigious *Journal of Contemporary Photography.* His work was included in the Cleveland Museum of Art's 1994 Invitational and 1996 "Legacy of Light: Master Photographs from the Cleveland Museum of Art" as well as the 2001 "Full Beard, Long Hair ... The Image of Jesus Christ in Photography, 1839–2001," in Germany.

Douglas Phillips (1922–1995): *Christ Called Mankind,* 1991, stained-glass window; *Burning Bush,* 1961, stained-glass screen (photographs by Mona Phillips).

Douglas Phillips and his wife, Mona Phillips, worked side by side in his own studio (established in 1952) for more than forty years designing and executing stained-glass art for churches of every denomination, in and out of the region, developing an extensive portfolio of classic though contemporary paintings, icons, and mosaics. Many of these commissions received awards for design, lighting, and craftsmanship.

Playhouse Square: Allen Theater Auditorium Restoration, 1998, GSI Architects, Inc. (photograph by Marc Braun), Playhouse Square Foundation.

Of the few surviving movie palaces in the country, four of them that stand side-by-side have been restored and preserved in one of the most unique complexes of theaters. The Playhouse Square complex of four theaters (Palace, State, Ohio, and Allen) is the largest theater complex between New York City and Chicago. These theaters, originally built in 1921, have been completely renovated and are being used for local and national theater and entertainment.

Horace Potter (1873–1948): jewelry designs, ca. 1940s: moonstone and diamond bracelet; cameo and pearls; sapphire, diamond, and yellow-gold bracelet, Potter and Mellen, Inc.

Educated at the Cleveland School of Art and at the Boston Society of Arts and Crafts, Horace Potter furthered his study in Europe in design and enameling and by learning from such mentor-colleagues as Louis Rorimer and R Guy Cowan. The generation of Frederick Miller and John Paul Miller gained expertise directly from his counsel.

Angelica Pozo (b. 1954): *Market Place/Meeting Place: An Urban Memorial,* with Penny Rakoff, 1994, mosaic tile bench with photographic decals and historic artifacts, 18' x 25' x 7'.

Pozo works full time as a ceramic artist and in the Ohio Arts Council's Artists-in-Education program. She has also taught tile making at the Penland School of Crafts and the Haystack Mountain School of Crafts and architectural ceramics at the Cleveland Institute of Art. She worked with Penny Rakoff to create this piece to commemorate the old Central Market area that gave way to the Gateway complex. The tiles are captioned photographic images; the mosaic frieze around the base exhibits the market produce. Her other public art installations are at RTA stops at Cleveland Hopkins International Airport and on East 9th Street.

Penny Rakoff (b. 1951): *Nightscape on the Cuyahoga #1,* 1987, Ektacolor print, 14¾" x 18⅞", Akron Art Museum, purchased with funds donated by Beatrice K. McDowell.

Rakoff is a professor at the University of Akron. Most of her public art pieces include photographic imagery. This work has a surreal tone and uses light, reflection, ambiguity, and stillness; a mood study of the river, it is both realistic and ethereal. Rakoff has received many awards, and her work is included in private and public collections, including the George Eastman International Museum of Photography in Rochester, New York, the Museum of Fine Arts in Houston, the Museum of Contemporary Photography in Chicago, and the Cleveland Museum of Art.

Louis Rorimer (1872–1939): Table and chair designed for the Silver Grille, 1931, Higbee Company, Forest City Enterprises.

Louis Rorimer was a lynchpin for activity in design—architectural, interior, and furniture. He had the ear of the patrons as owner of the Rorimer Brooks Company and taught decorative arts and design at the Cleveland Institute of Art from 1898 until 1936. Among his students were Horace Potter, Max Kalish, and Charles Burchfield. He drew on the synergism that could be forged among these disciplines, particularly important at a time when the opportunities for artist-architect collaboration were prime.

Rose Iron Works: *Art Deco Screen,* 1930, designed by Paul Feher, wrought iron and brass with silver and gold plating, 61.5" x 61.5", loaned to the Cleveland Museum of Art by the Rose Family Collection.

This screen is a prime example of the quality of design and craftsmanship that has come from Rose Iron Works since the turn of the twentieth century. Other examples have become part of our visual vocabulary as we see them along the wall at the former entryway of the Cleveland Botanical Gardens or dividing screens in the old Halle department store.

Charles Louis Sallee Jr. (b. 1914): *Anna,* ca. 1936, oil on canvas, 43" x 33", Dr. Albert C. Antoine and Mrs. June Sallee Antoine.

Charles Sallee, who apprenticed with his father, an ornamental plasterer, had many assignments during the WPA period, when he was a vigorous painter and printmaker at the Karamu WPA Printmaking Project. Among his life works are the interior design commissions at the Cleveland Stadium and the Grand Ballroom at the Stouffer's Inn-on-the-Square (now Renaissance Cleveland Hotel).

Judith Salomon (b. 1952): *Platters,* 2001, white earthenware clay, 23" round x 3½" depth, University Hospitals Chagrin Headlands Medical Center.

This earthenware work is distinctive in its imaginative shapes, vibrant color, and aggressive size. Salomon has taught ceramics at the Cleveland Institute of Art since 1977. Her work has been collected worldwide and noted in more than twenty publications. It can be seen in many public and private collections as well as in more than two dozen shows, national and international. Her work is included in the permanent collections of the Victoria and Albert Museum in London, the Los Angeles County Museum of Art, and the Lannan Foundation in Los Angeles. A ceramics teacher at the Cleveland Institute of Art since 1977, Salomon has received grants from the National Endowment for the Arts and the Ohio Arts Council and has enjoyed lectureships around the world. She received the Cleveland Arts Prize in 1990.

Fred Schmidt (1936–2001): *Freedom Dance,* 2000, painted metal, 44" x 23½" x 73½", Cleveland Clinic.

Fred Schmidt came from a rural and industrial background. He learned to weld when he worked for the New York Central Railroad in the early 1960s. During lunch hours

he began to fashion sculptures from scraps of steel. Over many years he developed his own personal style that explored and exploited the strength and flexibility of the material. He created elegant pieces like this one that seem to twist in space. He also created rough-looking sculptures of found objects. This piece is located at the Cleveland Clinic Children's Hospital for Rehabilitation. Schmidt's works have been widely exhibited and are in private and corporate collections, including the *Cleveland Plain Dealer,* University Hospitals, and Penn Central.

Viktor Schreckengost (b. 1906): Victor among his pedal cars, 1959, created from scraps of metal from automobile manufacturers; *Early Settler,* 1955, ceramic terra-cotta sculpture, 18' x 34' (photograph by Berni Rich).

Viktor Schreckengost was celebrated by the Cleveland Museum of Art with the 2000 exhibit "Viktor Schreckengost and Twentieth Century Design." A true Renaissance man, he is a ceramist, painter, sculptor, and teacher. As head of the Industrial Design Department at the Cleveland Institute of Art from 1930 until the late 1990s, he had tremendous influence on his students, who have continued his legacy. His design philosophy has been important to the automotive and toy industries most particularly. He has won many local and national awards for his work and has exhibited in the Paris Expo, New York's Metropolitan Museum of Art, and the Whitney Museum of American Art.

Phyllis Seltzer (b. 1928): *Dichotomy (L),* 2000, Ed 10, heat-transfer print, 50" x 38", State of Ohio Office Building, Columbus.

This artist has maintained a traditional approach toward her recognizable subject matter and has been an innovator as a printmaker. For more than twenty years her heat-transfer method has produced works of vibrant color. Beginning with a painting created with stabilo pencil and oil paint that acts as the plate, Seltzer divides the completed painting into sizes compatible with the imagery and the size of the newspaper. The plate is then laid on the laser copier and sheets of heat-transfer paper are run through the machine. This paper is coated with a special emulsion that absorbs and holds the colors via an electrically charged field.

Severance Hall: 1930, architectural plans, Walker and Weeks, architects (photograph by Roger Mastroianni).

Severance Hall is home of the Cleveland Orchestra. Built in 1930 and opened in 1931, the concert hall was donated by John L. Severance as a memorial to his wife Elizabeth DeWitt Severance. Henry Hering was the sculptor of the relief work on the pediments and Elsa Vick Shaw was the artist commissioned to do the murals in the rotunda.

Shaker Square (1927–29): The second-oldest outdoor shopping development in the country, Shaker Square is listed in the National Register of Historic Places. It recently underwent complete renovation to stimulate the revival of a commercial complex as originally envisioned with a mix of specialty and service stores, restaurants, banks, and coffee shops.

Phyllis Sloane (b. 1921): *Still Life with Still Life Drawings,* 1987, acrylic on canvas, 48" x 54"; *Paul Travis,* 1970, serigraph, 29¼" x 25½", Cleveland Artists Foundation, gift of the artist.

Phyllis Sloane creates arrangements of shapes and patterns that surround studies of people and settings. Using several art media, she has been a painter (and especially enjoys working with watercolor) and a printmaker (cork cuts, linoleum cuts, woodcuts, silk screen, serigraphs, heat transfer, and etching), and her drawing is highly skilled and has focused many times on people in our midst or settings we recognize. The work, colorful and uplifting, has been commissioned by private and public patrons. She has exhibited in Columbus, Boston, Santa Fe, Philadelphia, and frequently at the Cleveland Museum of Art's May Show. A recipient of many awards, she received the Cleveland Arts Prize in the Visual Arts in 1982.

William Sommer (1867–1949): *Bach Chord,* 1923, oil on board, 20" x 23¾", Akron Art Museum, gift of Russell Munn in memory of Helen G. Munn; *The City in 1833,* 1934, mural (photograph by Don Snyder), Cleveland Public Library.

William Sommer's work has become widely recognized more recently. He was active among the region's artists as a teacher and mentor as well as the leader of the Kokoon Arts Club (1911–46), whose members met often to draw and paint, exhibit and celebrate. Brandywine, in the northwest corner of Northfield Township, was Sommer's "retreat" for himself and his friends. Sommer leaves a legacy of vibrant portrait and scene paintings in light hues and with elegant strokes of drawing genius.

Julian Stanczak (b. 1928): *City Mural,* 1973, 12-story fresco.

Identified early in his career as an up-and-coming talent in the realm of perceptual abstraction, Julian Stanzcak has reflected on and painted with highly developed techniques involving form and color. He has been recognized nationally and internationally with solo exhibits and retrospectives, and he has been written about in books and catalogues. He

taught for thirty-eight years at the Cleveland Institute of Art. This mural, on the Carter Manor Building, is one of ten painted on city walls in the mid-1970s as part of the Cleveland Area Arts Council's City Canvases project.

Athena Tacha (b. 1936): *Tension Arches,* 1975, painted stainless steel, 12' x 24' x 2', Cleveland State University.

Athena Tacha is a pioneer in the field of site sculpture. Her public career started with this piece commissioned by the Cleveland Area Arts Council in celebration of the country's Bicentennial. Now her sculpture can be found in more than thirty locations throughout the United States including two pieces on Bellflower Road on the Case Western Reserve University campus. Tacha, a professor of sculpture at Oberlin College from 1973 to 1998, has had more than fifteen solo exhibits of her work and a retrospective at the High Museum in Atlanta in 1989; she has also been included in more than fifty group shows. She is the recipient of numerous awards, including a National Endowment for the Arts grant in 1975 and an Ohio Arts Council individual artist fellowship in 1991, and has been the subject of many articles and essays.

Toshiko Takaezu (b. 1922): *Star Series,* 1999–2000, 11 pieces, glazed stoneware, to 67" x 28" x 28" diameter, Racine Art Museum, gift of the artist.

Toshiko Takaezu has taught at numerous schools, including the Cleveland Institute of Art, Penland School of Crafts, and Princeton University, and has received numerous awards and honors. A 1975 fellow of the American Craft Council and 1994 recipient of an American Craft Council gold medal award for artistic excellence, she has had more than twenty solo exhibitions. Her work is represented in the collections of the Smithsonian Institution, the Museum of Fine Arts in Boston, the Philadelphia Museum of Art, the Detroit Institute of Arts, and in more than fifteen other museums and art centers in this country and abroad.

Paul Travis (1891–1975): *Summers Harvest,* ca. 1917, watercolor, 18" x 22" (photograph by Berni Rich), Elaine and Joseph Kisvardai; *The Syndics,* 1946, oil on masonite, 31½" x 50", Cleveland Artists Foundation, gift of Elisabeth and Michael Dreyfuss.

When Paul Travis was a student at the Cleveland School of Art, his teacher Henry Keller emphasized the importance of observation and drawing. After serving in World War I, Travis extended his tour of duty and sketched and painted what he saw. On his return in 1920 he began his teaching career at the Cleveland School of Art, where he was one of the region's most beloved teachers for almost forty years. He is remembered for his 1928 trip to paint in Africa with funds from the Gilpin Players of Karamu House, and he brought back paintings that were shown in Cleveland and Milwaukee. He exhibited in group shows at the Carnegie Institute of Art in Pittsburgh and the Art Institute of Chicago. There was a solo exhibition of his work at the Butler Art Institute in Youngstown, Ohio, in 1943. His work was shown in fifty May Shows.

Brinsley Tyrrell (b. 1941): *Salt of the City,* 1996 and 2000, salt sculpture, SPACES.

Most of Brinsley Tyrrell's work for the past ten years has been related to his public art projects. Interested in the properties of salt and salt's role in Cleveland's natural and industrial landscape (the largest salt mine in North America lies under Lake Erie), he sculpted *Salt of the City* for "Urban Evidence" out of two large quarried boulders of salt mounted on top of a sandstone block on a concrete pedestal. He left the piece for nature to carve. Nearly a decade later, nature is still carving beautiful spiky forms and leaving brine deposits on the sandstone. An emeritus professor of art at Kent State University, Tyrrell has had numerous solo exhibitions in Ohio and has been selected for group exhibits in New York and Los Angeles.

Lilian Tyrrell (b. 1944): *Poisonous Legacy,* 1990, tapestry, linen and silk, 58' x 117", Progressive Corporation.

With technical brilliance, Lilian Tyrrell's large-scale tapestries—like fiber paintings—confront the viewer with some of society's pressing and provocative issues. In *Poisonous Legacy,* a comment on pollution, an oversized figure covered with cloth and using a breathing tube looks at us from a devastated landscape. Tyrrell's work has been exhibited in Alaska, Portland, Maine, and Toronto, among many places. She was included in the Cleveland Museum of Art's 1994 Invitational, and her installation for "Urban Evidence: Contemporary Artists Reveal Cleveland" was exhibited at SPACES.

Douglas Max Utter (b. 1950): *The World Long Ago,* 1991, mixed paint media on canvas, 66" x 50".

Over the past two decades the subjects of Utter's works have been either iconographic or deeply personal. Often working with unconventional paint media like latex house paint, spray paint, or various asphalt commercial substances, his portraits of family members and close friends often refer to Christian or neo-classical concerns. His work has been

shown in more than 100 exhibitions, including twenty one-person shows in Cleveland, Augsberg, Germany, New York, Phoenix, and Los Angeles. He has received Ohio Arts Council Fellowships in Painting and Art Criticism. His essays and reviews have appeared in six publications, and he is senior editor of *Angle,* a non-profit journal of arts and culture.

Sandor Vago (1887–1946): *Self-Portrait,* 1937, oil on canvas, 32¼" x 28", Cleveland Museum of Art, presented by the Friends of the Artist.

Upon emigrating from Europe in the early part of the century, Vago opened a studio and developed a thriving career as a portrait painter. His expressive and painterly style earned him many commissions, and he worked for such institutions as the Western Reserve Academy, the Catholic Diocese of Cleveland, the Musical Arts Association, the General Electric Corporation, and Cleveland City Hall. He exhibited in more than twenty-five May Shows and had solo exhibitions in the leading galleries of the time. He taught at the Cleveland School of Art from 1929 to 1935.

van Dijk, Westlake, Reed, and Leskosky: Blossom Music Center, 1968, architect Peter Van Dijk (b. 1929), photograph by Bruce Kiefer); Nathan and Fanny Shafran Planetarium at the Cleveland Museum of Natural History, 2002, architect Paul Westlake (b. 1952), photograph by Nick Merrick Hedrich Blessing; facade of Society National Bank, 1992, photograph by Gary Quesada and Justin Maconochie; lamp restoration, Society National Bank, 1989–91, photograph by Gary Quesada and Justin Maconochie; facade of Federal Reserve Bank, 1996, photograph by Gary Quesada and Justin Maconochie.

Van Dijk, Westlake, Reed, and Leskosky was founded in 1905 by Abram Garfield, the son of President James Garfield, and is the oldest continually operating architectural firm in northern Ohio. With a professional staff of nearly 100, the firm maintains an average volume of $500 million in projects in design and construction. The aesthetic upon which they have gained their reputation is grace and elegance. Shapes tend to be unusual yet classical, quiet rather than pushing space aggressively. The firm has been honored with more than 100 significant design awards in the last twenty-five years, including the AIA Ohio Gold Medal Firm Award and several honors from the National Trust for Historic Preservation. Their work has been extensively featured in professional and popular publications, including *Architecture, Architectural Record, Progressive Architecture,* and *Interiors.*

Laila Voss (b. 1952): *A Chaotic Symphony: The Catch-All Net*, 1996, raw and recycled materials.

Laila Voss was the only artist whose installation appeared at all of the exhibit sites for "Urban Evidence: Contemporary Artists Reveal Cleveland": the Cleveland Museum of Art, the Center for Contemporary Art (now Museum of Contemporary Art Cleveland), and SPACES. For this piece she collected refuse from natural and consumer materials found as she followed the Cuyahoga River through Cleveland. Gathered in huge nets, the "raw and recycled materials" provide a portrait of the city, with each site offering different materials, a different view. Voss's installations emphasized a theme of the entire exhibition, which was that history is not a prepared set of facts but a fabric woven from available elements.

Frank Wilcox (1887–1964): *Twilight*, ca. 1932, watercolor, 18" x 22" (photograph by Berni Rich), Elaine and Joseph Kisvardai; *Along Canal Street, Cleveland,* ca. 1960, zinc plate etching (photograph by Berni Rich), Elaine and Joseph Kisvardai; *The General Store,* ca. 1930, watercolor, pencil, and gouache on paper, 21½" x 29¼", Hahn Loeser & Parks LLP; *Brecksville Stage Coach Inn,* ca. 1930, watercolor, gouache on paper, Hahn Loeser & Parks LLP.

Frank Wilcox was most famous for his watercolors. He was a reporter in words and drawing and painting. Perhaps most important to him was the record of Ohio—its countryside, canals, and all of the Indian trails drawn and painted with love and clarity. He personally researched miles and miles of canals and towpaths and recreated an imagined past and the ways of the industrial, agricultural, and economic growth of the region. In 1913 he joined mentors Frederick Gottwald, Henry Keller, and Louis Rorimer on the faculty of the Cleveland School of Art, where he taught drawing, painting, design, and printmaking for forty years to students like Carl Gaertner and Charles Burchfield. He traveled to Europe and to the Armory Show in New York City, where he absorbed the new European aesthetic. He won more than thirty awards in the May Show and won the 1920 Penton Medal for sustained excellence. His work was exhibited widely, including in the Art Institute of Chicago, the Museum of Modern Art, and the Whitney Museum of American Art in New York City.

Brent Kee Young (b. 1946): *Fossil Series. "Worlds . . . Apart,"* 1993, blown glass and 23K gold leaf, carved bass wood base, ca. 15" x 10".

Brent Kee Young has been a professor of glass art at the Cleveland Institute of Art since 1973. His work transforms glass into objects of art using abstract ideas and mostly recognizable forms. He fuses the traditional craft of glassmaking with contemporary form. He has had solo exhibitions in the United States and Japan. His work is included in several dozen national and international exhibits and is in the collection of the Corning Museum of Glass, the High Museum of Art in Atlanta, the Art Institute of Chicago, and the Lanning Foundation in Los Angeles, as well as other private and corporate collections.

Appendix B: Artists' Matters

Cleveland Arts Prize in Architecture and the Visual Arts

Architecture
The J. Milton Dyer Memorial Award

1962	J. Byers Hays
1965	Robert A. Little
1965	Fred S. Toguchi
1968	John Terence Kelly
1969	Peter Van Dyjk
1970	Don Hisaka
1972	Philip Johnson
1973	Norman K. Perttula
1974	Richard Fleischman
1978	William Trout
1983	William B. Morris
1985	Blunden Barclay
1988	Lesko Associates
1990	Stephen J. Bucchieri
1995	Paul Westlake Jr.
2001	Ronald A. Reed
2002	Thom Stauffer
2003	Vince Leskosky

Visual Arts

1961	John Paul Miller, goldsmith
1962	Toshiko Takaezu, potter
1963	Kenneth Bates, enamelist
1964	William McVey, sculptor
1965	Paul Travis, painter
1966	Ed Mieczkowski, painter
1967	John Clague, sculptor
1968	Fredrick A. Miller, silversmith
1969	Julian Stanczak, painter
1970	Joseph McCullough, painter
1971	H. C. Cassill, printmaker
1972	Clarence H. Carter, painter
1973	Viktor Schreckengost, industrial designer and painter
1974	Joseph B. O'Sickey, painter
1975	John Pearson, painter
1977	Richard Anuszkiewicz, painter
1978	Ralph Woehrman, painter-printmaker
1979	Hugh Kepets, painter
1980	David E. Davis, sculptor
1981	Athena Tacha, sculptor
1982	Phyllis Sloane, painter-printmaker
1983	Claude Conover, ceramist
1984	Wenda F. Von Weise, quilt tapestry
1985	Moe Brooker, painter
1986	Shirley Aley Campbell, painter
1987	Brent Kee Young, glass artist
1988	Kenneth Nevadomi, painter
1989	Carl Floyd, sculptor
1990	Judith Salomon, ceramist
1991	Don Harvey, sculptor
1992	Lilian Tyrrell, weaver
1993	La Wilson, sculptor
1994	Masumi Hayashi, photographer
1995	John L. Moore, painter
1997	Kenneth Dingwall, painter
1998	Holly Morrison, visual artist
1999	Linda Butler, photographer

2000 Laurence Channing, graphic artist
2001 George Fitzpatrick, painter
2002 Christina DePaul, artist
2003 Johnny Coleman, sound and installation sculptor

Index of Ceramic Artists in Cleveland Museum of Art May Show 1958–1993
Compiled by William Busta

The catalog for the 1958 May Show (40th in the series) was the first to list all artists in the show by category. The last May Show was in 1993 (72nd in the series). Exhibitions were not held in 1970, 1991, and 1992.

The bold-faced codes after exhibition years indicate that a special award was given:

HP   Horace E. Potter Memorial Award for Excellence in Craftsmanship
1st etc. Place Awards
HM   Prize (only in 1958); Honorable Mention (all other years)
JM   Jury Mention, Juror's Mention
SM   Special Mention, Special Mention for Crafts
SJM   Special Jury Mention
$1000   Crafts $1000 Award (some were split, ½ $1000)
C$500   Robert Mann Award for Ceramics
C$1000   Robert Mann Award for Ceramics

Karen S. Acker   1983
William M. Aigner   1964
Sandra Amitay   1977 **$1000**, 1978, 1979 **SM**, 1980 **SM**, 1981, 1982, 1985, **C$500**, 1986, 1987 **C$500**, 1990, 1993
Doris C. Andrie   1972
Jill Angelovic   1990
John J. Antolik   1958
Jean E. Appleby   1973, 1977, 1987
Elizabeth Ash   1958, 1959, 1960, 1965
Sandra M. August   1961, 1964
Leonard A. Backiel, Adela Backiel   1958
Tom Balbo   1976, 1987
Donald Barone   1976 **SM**
William D. Barron   1975
Nicole Bastide   1980, 1981
David Batz   1971, 1972 **SM**, 1973, 1974, 1975, 1977, 1978, 1979, 1980, 1986, 1987, 1993
Judith Beasley   1967
Albert Beck   1965
Judy Bennett   1988

Teri Benton   1974
Curtis Benzle   1972, 1979
Curtis and Suzan Benzle   1981 ½ **$1000**
Diane Bjel   1973
Eric L. Blecher   1975, 1978
Mary Jo Bole   1985, 1988 **SM**
Gail S. Vandy Bogurt   1973, 1974, 1975 **$1000**
Bruce Bowers   1978, 1979, 1983, 1985
George Bowes   1987, 1989
Lucy Breslin   1983
A. Christopher Breuer   1984, 1985, 1988
Frances Brooke   1958
William Brouillard   1982, 1984, 1985
Joellen Bryan   1986
Olen Bryant   1958 **HM CS**
Stephen F. Bures   1984, 1986
Steve Burgess   1977
Patrick W. Burke   1983, 1985 **SM**, 1987, 1988
Dane Burr   1958
Martin L. Cader   1981
Donald Cahoo   1959
Jerome Caja   1981, 1984
Larry Calhoon   1972, 1975
Edith S. Carey   1958, 1960
Sean Carey   1987
Roy Cartwright   1964
Cristina Carver   1984 **C$500**
Edith S. Cary   1958, 1959, 1960, 1966
Kathleen Cerveny   1978
James G. Chaney   1973, 1975 **SM**
Gary Charpentier   1981
Denis Chasek   1960, 1964
Denis Chasek, with Jane Parshall   1958, 1962, 1964, 1965, 1966
Louise L. Cholfin, with Bruce Grimes   1968
Thomas Ciocia   1975, 1976, 1977
John Clague   1958, 1987
Sarah Clague   1959 **HM**, 1960, 1961
Sarah Reynolds Clague   1985, 1986
Kristen Cliffel   1990
Jacqueline A. Clipsham   1962
Kathryn E. Coble   1979
Ruta Cochran   1958 **3rd CS**
Elaine Albers Cohen   1962, 1965, 1969, 1986, 1987, 1989
Fern Cole   1971, 1974, 1975
Claude Conover   1959 **HM**, 1960 **3rd**, 1961 **JM**, 1962 **JM**, 1963 **JM**, 1964 **JM**, 1965 **JM**, 1966 **SM**, 1967, 1968 **SJM**, 1969, 1971, 1972, 1973
Ginny Conrow   1978, 1980, 1981, 1983, 1984
Anthony W. Corraro   1959, 1961

Mike Costello 1987

Maryann Cox 1984, 1985, 1988

Nancy Currier 1974, 1975

H. Robert Dague 1961

Loren J. D'Amore 1990

Myron Russell Davidson 1958, 1959, 1961, 1962, 1964, 1965
JM, 1966, 1968, 1971

Laurel Delia 1972

Paul F. Demeter 1960, 1961, 1963, 1964 JM, 1965, 1966, 1967,
1972, 1974, 1975, 1976 SM

Ron Desmett 1974, 1977

Delpha Dickson 1966, 1967 JM, 1969

Janice Sue Diller 1976, 1979

Paul Stanley Dominey 1965

Berard G. Donatucci 1963

Bette Drake 1964, 1967, 1972, 1981, 1983, 1987

Paula Dubaniewicz 1978, 1979, 1980

Gerald Dumlao 1963, 1964

Jerry Dunnigan 1966

Norita Eglet 1964

Letitia Eldredge 1968 $1000

Cathleen E. Elliott 1981

Judith Eilmann 1960

Jane E. Engle 1961

Michael J. Evans (collaborators Mr. and Mrs. Evans Jr.) 1978

Sheri Okum Farbstein 1976, 1977 SM, 1980

Dorothy E. Fasig 1967, 1968

Maybelle Muttart Falardeau 1958, 1959

Christine Federighi 1972

Marcy Feren 1977, 1978

Cleo Bell Ferguson 1962, 1963, 1964, 1967, 1968

Florence Y. Fillous 1965

Nancy Y. Finesilver 1973, 1975, 1978, 1984, 1988

Millie Firak 1972

Jean Fleshler 1983

Daniel James Forst 1958

Rhonda D. Franklin 1990

Matilda Fusek 1960

Herbert T. Fyhr 1962, 1963, 1965, 1967

Herbert T. Fyhr (collaborator Maude Fyhr) 1964

Sally Schwerzler Gaetjens 1960

Marian Royce Gage 1959

Susan M. Gallagher 1990

Maryann T. Gallowitz 1962, 1964, 1965, 1966

Gene Gant 1968, 1971

Clark Garnsey 1958

Melissa Gaskins 1989

Vance Van Drake Gedeon 1958, 1959

Christine Gederighi 1972

Gabor Gergo 1960, 1961, 1962, 1964, 1965, 1966, 1967

Ken Gessford 1971, 1972, 1974

Barbara Giesel 1975

Suzanne Gilbert 1975, 1984, 1985

Doug Gilliam 1985 SM, 1987

Clement C. Giorgi 1958, 1959 HM, 1960, 1961, 1962, 1966

David C. Giorgi 1958, 1959, 1960, 1961, 1963, 1966, 1967

Fern M. Giorgi 1958 1st CS

Judith Ann Glezen 1959

Larry Goebelt 1989

Gwen-Lin Goo 1968

Bonnie J. Gordon 1982, 1983, 1984, 1985, 1986, 1987, 1988,
1989, 1990, 1993

M. E. Goslee 1958 2nd CS, 1960, 1962, 1963, 1964, 1965 JM,
1971, 1972

Janet Grau 1990

Vicki B. Graves 1960

Maureen Gregory 1958

Stefani Gruenberg 1961

Maija Gruzitis 1966

Michael Gubkin 1984, 1985, 1987, 1988, 1989

George Hageman 1967

Margaret Handel 1978

Margarita Handel 1988

Gary Hart 1971

Daniel M. Heekin 1978

Jean Moodey Heffter 1958

Gary V. Heider 1974

Annelies Heijnen 1986, 1987, 1988, 1989 $1000, 1993

Gary Henin 1973, 1974

Michael Hieber 1974

Nancy Himmel 1974, 1975, 1976

Kevin A. Hluch 1978, 1981, 1988

Ralph Hocking 1961

Margaret Hoffmann 1958, 1959, 1960, 1961, 1964, 1966, 1971,
1973, 1974

Ruth Ellen Hollingworth 1966 SM, 1967, 1969, 1971

Don Holzman 1990

Will Hubben 1981

Tom Huck 1985, 1989

Ronald Hules 1972

Barbara J. Humpage 1982, 1986, 1987, 1989

Harold Wesley Hunsicker 1959

Harold Wesley Hunsicker and Clarence Merritt 1958

Dorothy W. Icove 1983

Susan Icove 1983, 1984

Marlene Jack 1978, 1979

Ellen Janis 1962

Ann Selby Jeremiah 1984

Mark D. Johnson   1981, 1987, 1988

Thano A. Johnson   1958

Scott R. Jones   1984, 1987

Edward Kaplan   1976

Jonathan Kaplan   1971

Joyce E. Kaufman   1972

Kevin Kautenburger   1987, 1988, 1989 **C$1000**

George Kaye   1975, 1976

Sue Keebler   1977 **HP**, 1980, 1982, 1984, 1985 **SM**, 1986

Steven Kemenffy   1971, 1972 **$1000**

Susan B. Hale Kemenffy   1972 **SM**, 1975

Christine King   1976 **SM**, 1978

Jo Kirschenbaum   1978, 1983, 1985 **SM**

John Klassen   1978

David Kobak   1974, 1976

George C. Koch   1962

Greg Komp   1974, 1975

Howard W. Kottler   1960 **1st**, 1961 **JM**, 1962 **JM**, 1963 **JM**, 1964 **JM HP**, 1965, 1966, 1967 **JM**, 1968, 1969, 1971, 1972 **SM**, 1973 **HP**, 1974, 1975, 1976

Ronald Kowalyk   1969, 1973, 1990

Carl Richard Krabill   1960, 1961

Arthur R. Kuhl   1958

Karol Kuruc   1975 **SM**

Soon Hyung Kwan   1960

Eva Kwong   1990

Stanley Lake   1972, 1974, 1976, 1983

Charles Lakofsky   1958 **1st P**, 1959 **HM**, 1960, 1961, 1962 **JM**, 1963, 1964, 1965, 1966 **SM JM**, 1967 **SJM JM**, 1972, 1973, 1974, 1975

Louanne Lasdon   1974, 1976

Ann Jeremiah Legris   1988

Frances Lehnert   1973, 1974, 1980, 1984, 1987

Marty Levenson   1976, 1978

Ed Lewin   1977

Caren Liebert   1984

Luke and Rolland Lietzke   1961, 1963, 1967

Beth E. Lindenberger   1986, 1988, 1989

Richard J. Linenau   1960

Robert Lucas   1963

Gregory N. Lucic   1974 ½ **$1000**

Winifred Lutz   1967

Eleanor Madonik   1971, 1974

Marcia Madonik   1974

Dorathee G. Manbeckv   1959

Norman E. Magden   1958 **HM**, 1960, 1961, 1962

Jerome Malinowski   1961

Catherine Malloy   1958, 1960, 1961, 1962, 1963, 1964, 1965, 1967, 1969, 1976

Dorathee G. Manbeck   1958 **2nd P**, 1959, 1961, 1962

Betty Jean Manichl   1976

Tim Mather and Annette McCormick   1987

Alan R. Maxwell   1976, 1978

Alan R. Maxwell (collaborator Sandy Davis)   1975

Alan R. Maxwell (collaborator Bill Jones)   1975

Mary M. Maxwell   1974, 1977

Sandra May   1965

Richard Allen Mayer   1972

Annette McCormick   1980

Elizabeth C. McFadyen   1958, 1959 (First Prize [1st?]), 1961, 1963, 1964, 1966

Leza McVey   1958 **3rd C**, 1959, 1960, 1961 **JM**, 1962, 1963, 1964, 1965 **JM**, 1966, 1967, 1968, 1969

Louie Meier   1964

Honey Meir-Levi   1984

Lance A. Meneghelli   1965

Marjo Meyers   1958, 1959, 1960, 1961

Milan Mihalek   1987

Robert Mihaly   1976, 1977, 1978, 1979, 1982, 1984, 1989, 1990

Paul Miklowski   1979, 1980 **SM**, 1981, 1983 **$1000**, 1984, 1986, 1987 **C$500**

Steve Mikola 1965, 1966, 1967

D. Joseph Mikolay   1958 **HM**, 1959, 1960, 1963

Elayne S. Miller   1973

Gary E. Miller   1974 **SM**, 1975

Joy Miller   1971, 1972

Richard L. Miller   1960

Lorna Minich   1978, 1983

Hugh Moore   1958

Aann Morris   1958

Helene S. Morse   1980

Sherwin Moss   1972, 1973, 1974 **SM**, 1976

Jack Matthew Moulthrop   1986, 1987, 1989, 1993

Alan Myers   1971 **SM**, 1972, 1973, 1976

Ardys Nichols   1966, 1968

Joan Nordstrom   1980

Elizabeth Nutt   1964

Beverly O'Brien   1985, 1986

Norma Olsen   1966, 1967

Arlene Olson   1969, 1971

Mary C. L. Organ   1990 **SM**

Nobuko Otsuki   1962

Gerri Palmer   1985, 1987, 1993

George W. Palovich   1962, 1966, 1974

Janet E. Palovich   1962 **JM**

Jane Parshall   1960, 1962, 1963, 1964, 1965

Jane Parshall (collaborators Denis Chasek and Arden Riddle)   1966

Mark Passerell   1971, 1972

Vernon Patrick   1967

Neil J. Patterson   1988 ½ C$1000

Scott N. Pergande   1986, 1990

James D. Peters   1960, 1961, 1962

Miska F. Petersham   1961, 1963 JM, 1964, 1965, 1969

Greg Pitts   1982

Joyce Porcelli   1980, 1981

Daniel T. Postotnik   1984, 1985, 1987, 1988, 1990, 1993

Angelica Pozo   1987 SM, 1988, 1989 SM, 1993 C$1000

Joy Elaine Praznik   1961, 1962, 1963, 1964, 1965, 1966, 1967
   SJM, 1971, 1972, 1973, 1977, 1984, 1987

Andrea Garson Preis 1990

Marian Pritchard   1984

G. W. Rareshield   1989, 1990

Darl Rastorfer   1973

Sarah E. Reynolds   1958

Mike Ribar   1973

Jo Rice   1960

Carol Pickands Richard   1958

Jennie Robbins   1971

Richard Robishaw   1974, 1975

George A. Roby   1964, 1965, 1966, 1967 JM, 1969, 1971, 1972,
   1973, 1974, 1975 SM, 1976 SM, 1977, 1978 SM, 1979 $1000,
   1980 SM, 1981, 1982

Joanna Rodono (Rodono-Brown 1967)   1961, 1962, 1964, 1967

Mary-Lyell Rogers   1958

Christina Root   1989

Yetta Rosenberg   1959

Jack Rotar   1977, 1989

George Sacco   1974, 1975

Frank Safranek   1961

Judith Salomon   1979, 1980, 1981, 1983, 1985, 1986, 1989, 1990
   $1000, 1993

Flora Wayne Sargous   1958, 1959, 1961, 1967

Lorri Sarosy   1976, 1977, 1983

Sue Sauvageau   1973

Michael S. Schick   1978

Larry Schiemann   1976

Gary A. Schlappal   1977 SM, 1978 $1000, 1981 SM, 1982,
   1983, 1985, 1987, 1988, 1990 HP

JoAnn Schnabel   1988, 1990

Carolyn Schnedarek   1958, 1959

Patricia Hiughes Schneider   1982, 1983, 1985, 1986 C$500,
   1987, 1988

Richard D. Schneider   1974, 1975, 1977, 1978, 1979, 1980, 1981,
   1982, 1983 SM, 1984, 1985, 1986, 1987, 1988 ½ C$1000

Ella A. Schrock   1958, 1960, 1961, 1962, 1964, 1966

Susan K. P. Schroeder   1976

Caroline Schwerzler   1962

Gary Stuart Schwerzler   1963, 1964, 1967

Josephine Scranton   1959, 1960, 1961, 1962

Barbara Seletzky   1958

Andrea Serafino   1985

Kathleen Totter Sheldon   1968, 1972, 1975

Elizabeth S. Shelton   1958, 1959, 1961, 1963, 1964

Edgar H. Simon   1973

Ann Simmons   1966

Susan M. Sipos   1977, 1978, 1979, 1988, 1989

J. Paul Sires   1977, 1978, 1979 SM

David P. Skeggs   1968

Phyllis Sloane   1965

Peter Adam Slusarksi   1961

Penny Smith   1990

Vincent L. Soldacki   1980

James M. Someroski   1958, 1961

George J. Somogyi   1974 SM, 1975

Lisa Sorokach   1976

Richard Spangle   1962, 1963, 1964, 1967, 1971, 1973, 1974, 1975

Carl R. Staub   1976

John H. Stephenson   1959

Norman Ray Stewart   1963, 1964

Frank Susi   1973, 1974, 1976

Sanford J. Sussman   1971

Mary Ann Svec   1975

Frederick Sweet   1974

Toshiko Takaezu   1958 HP, 1959, 1960 2nd, 1961, 1962 JM,
   1963 JM, 1964 JM, 1965, 1966 SM

Barbara Takiguchi   1973

Diana Taylor   1981

Mel Tearle   1975

Barbara Tiso   1967

Elaine Triana   1967

Janet E. Trisler   1965 JM, 1973

Jack Troy   1967, 1971

Richard L. Tschantz   1974

J. Kay Turk   1962

Andrea Vaiksnoras Uravitch   1988

Elaine Lowery Urban   1958, 1959

Ted G. Urban   1958

Lin Vajner   1984, 1985

Blanche Vanis   1958

David Vargo   1977, 1979, 1980, 1981, 1984, 1985, 1986, 1987

Mike Vatalaro   1972 SM, 1973, 1974

Kenneth Vavrek   1965, 1966, 1967 $1000 SJM JM, 1968, 1969,
   1971, 1972

Dolores Chatham Vazquez   1964, 1965, 1966

Helen Vedensky   1958, 1960

David W. Veit   1958
William R. Vokolek   1961, 1963, 1964
Nijole Bartuska Von Kiparski   1988
Michael T. Ward   1989
Varda E. Washington   1962
James Watral   1965, 1966
Donna S. Webb   1977, 1979, 1984, 1985, 1987, 1988, 1990
James Weckbacher   1983, 1984, 1988, 1989
Jamie Weiss   1972
Jerry F. Weiss   1963, 1964
Thomas Rolf Weissenberg   1965
John Wenzel   1967
S. Judson Wilcox   1985
Diane Bjel Wilks   1985, 1986
Edward W. Willard   1961, 1964
David E. Williamson   1978, 1979, 1981, 1982
Susan H. Wilson   1982
Ellen Wohl   1977
George Woideck   1987
Josephine Wood   1980, 1981
Robert B. Yost   1988, 1990 **C$1000**
Joan Zalenski   1968

Joseph R. Zeller   1971, 1972, 1973
Robert Zerlin   1958
Nancy Zick   1985
Katsue Zimmerman   1989
Catherine Zurchin   1984
Marilyn Zurmuehlen   1966 **SM**

Compiler's Note: When a name was listed in the May Show catalogs in several variants, the longest form is used here. For example, if a middle initial was ever used, it is included. If "Thomas" was ever listed, it is used here instead of Tom (even if Tom is more frequent). In case of any doubt of identity, names are listed separately. When more than one name is listed for a piece, the association between the two artists is indicated here using the same linkage words that were used in the catalogs ("collaboration," "with," etc.). However, if two artists worked together on pieces over time, and the May Show used different "association" words, editorial discretion was used to select one choice for this index.

The Cleveland Museum of Art now has a complete database of the May Show exhibits available on its website.

Appendix C: University Circle Walking Tour Map

Map Key, Alphabetical

38 African American Museum
71 Alcazar
69 Ambleside Towers
58 American Cancer Society
57 American Cancer Society Hope Lodge
59 American Heart Association
60 American Sickle Cell Anemia Association
65 Arabica
35 Baricelli Inn
66 Barking Spider
27 CaseWestern Reserve University
24 Case Amasa Stone Chapel
26 Case Art Studio Gallery
25 Case Eldred Theatre
70 Case Harkness Chapel
23 Case Mather Dance Center
19 Case Mather Gallery
53 Case's Peter B. Lewis building

61 Center for Dialysis Care
40 Children's Museum
45 Church of Jesus Christ of Latter-Day Saints
20 Church of the Covenant
12 Cleveland Botanical Garden
17 Cleveland Cinematheque
62 Cleveland Clinic
14 Cleveland Cultural Gardens
63 Cleveland Hearing & Speech
47 Cleveland Hillel Foundation
16 CIA Reinberger Galleries
15 Cleveland Institute of Art
10 Cleveland Institute of Music
1 Cleveland Museum of Art
6 Cleveland Museum of Natural History

8 Cleveland Music School Settlement
18 Cleveland Orchestra
48 Ceveland Play House
56 Cleveland Public Library
64 Cleveland Sight Center
49 Cleveland Signstage Theatre
32 Dittrick Medical History Museum
34 East 115th Street
3 Epworth-Euclid United Methodist Church
2 Fine Arts Garden
29 First Church of Christ, Scientist Building
39 Free Medical Clinic
54 Gestalt Institute of Cleveland
22 Glidden House
50 Hallinan Center
46 HealthSpace Cleveland
21 Hessler Road
36 Holy Rosary Church
68 InterContinental

Hotel & Conference Center
4 Judson Manor
28 Judson Park
51 Karamu Performing Arts Theatre
31 Lake View Cemetery
37 Little Italy Historical Museum
41 Louis Stokes Veterans Center
52 Lyric Opera Cleveland
44 Museum of Contemporary Art Cleveland
7 Mt. Zion Congregational Church
55 Ohio College of Podiatric Medicine
13 Pentecostal Church of Christ
42 Ronald McDonald House
30 Sculpture Center, The
67 Sergio's
5 Temple Tifereth-Israel
43 United Cerebral Palsy

By Greg Folly, 2002. Reprinted with permission from University Circle, Inc., and Live Publishing.

148

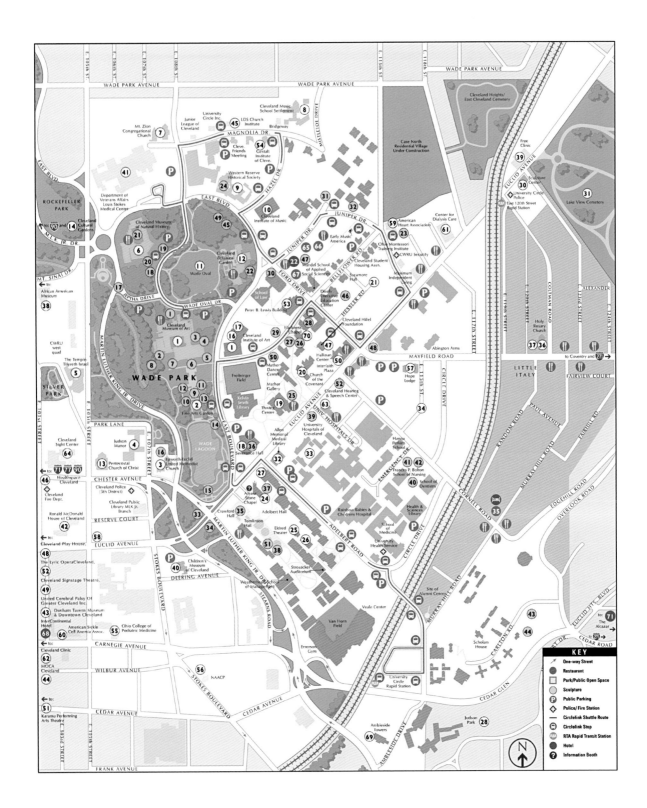

33 UniversityHospitals
11 Wade Oval
9 Western Reserve
   Historical Society

Map Key, Numerical

1 Cleveland Museum
  of Art
2 Fine Arts Garden
3 Epworth-Euclid
  United Methodist
  Church
4 Judson Manor
5 Temple Tifereth-
  Israel
6 Cleveland Museum
  of Natural History
7 Mt. Zion
  Congregational
  Church
8 Cleveland Music
  School Settlement
9 Western Reserve
  Historical Society
10 Cleveland Institute of
   Music
11 Wade Oval
12 Cleveland Botanical
   Garden
13 Pentecostal Church
   of Christ
14 Cleveland Cutural
   Gardens
15 Cleveland Institute of
   Art
16 CIA Reinberger
   Galleries
17 Cleveland
   Cinematheque
18 Cleveland Orchestra
19 Case Mather Gallery
20 Church of the
   Covenant
21 Hessler Road
22 Glidden House
23 Case Mather Dance
   Center
24 Case Amasa Stone
   Chapel
25 Case Eldred Theatre

26 Case Art Studio
   Gallery
27 Case Western Reserve
   University
28 Judson Park
29 First Church of
   Christ, Scientist
   Building
30 Sculpture Center
31 Lake View Cemetery
32 Dittrick Medical
   History Museum
33 University Hospitals
34 East 115th Street
35 Baricelli Inn
36 HolyRosaryChurch
37 Little Italy Historical
   Museum
38 African American
   Museum
39 Free Medical Clinic
40 Children's Museum
41 Louis Stokes Veterans
   Center
42 Ronald McDonald
   House
43 United Cerebral Palsy
44 MOCA Cleveland
45 Church of Jesus Christ
   of Latter-Day Saints
46 HealthSpace
   Cleveland
47 Cleveland Hillel
   Foundation
48 Cleveland Play House
49 Cleveland Signstage
   Theatre
50 Hallinan Center
51 Karamu Performing
   Arts Theatre
52 Lyric Opera
   Cleveland
53 Case's Peter B. Lewis
   Building
54 Gestalt Institute of
   Cleveland
55 Oho College of
   Podiatric Medicine
56 Cleveland Public
   Library

57 American Cancer
   Society Hope Lodge
58 American Cancer
   Society
59 American Heart
   Association
60 Amencan Sickle Cell
   Anemia Association
61 Center for Dialysis
   Care
62 Ceveland Clinic
63 Cleveland Hearing &
   Speech
64 Cleveland Sight
   Center
65 Arabica
66 Barking Spider
67 Sergio's
68 InterContinental
   Hotel & Conference
   Center
69 Ambleside Towers
70 Case Harkness
   Chapel
71 Alcazar

Sculpture Key

Sculpture is identified on
map by a numbered
yellow dot.

s1 Rock Carvings
s2 Warrior Borghese
s3 City Fettering Nature
s4 Harvey Rice
s5 Bacchanale
s6 The Thinker
s7 Boy with Panther Cub
s8 Tadeusz Kosciuszko
s9 Fountain of the
   Waters
s10 Sun
s11 Earth
s12 Twelve Signs of the
    Zodiac
s13 Spring Racing the
    Wind
s14 Mermaids
s15 Night Passing the
    Earth to Day

s16 Epworth-Euclid
    Church exterior
    sculpture
s17 General Milan R.
    Stefanik
s18 Stegosaurus
s19 Coursing Eagles
s20 Carolus Linnaeus
s21 Old Grizzly (Bruno
    the Bear)
s22 McDog
s23 Hart Crane
s24 Tom Johnson
s25 Snow Fence
s26 Sundial
s27 Merging
s28 Oeccan
s29 Twist
s30 Three Sculptures
    from "Alphabet
    Series"
s31 Back
s32 Start
s33 Marcus Hanna
s34 Louis Kossuth
    Monument
s35 Light Path Crossing
s36 Severance Hall
    pediment
s37 Morning Star 1982

s38 Spitball
s39 Wings of Eternity
s40 Coastlines
s41 Wayward Walls
s42 Desire to Heal
s43 Grid 14
s44 Unstable Tables
s45 Awakening
s46 Avignon
s47 Columns
s48 Euclid's Cirde
s49 Medusa
s50 Turnng Point Garden
s51 Michelson-Morley
    Fountain
s52 Stones

Appendix D: Participants in the Creative Essence Project

The Cleveland Artists Foundation community of board and staff, administrators, arts leaders, artists, presenters, and panelists for the series of dialogues are the core of Creative Essence: 1900–2000, the basis for the dialogue series, video production, website material, DVD content, and this publication. Also very important were the many hundreds in our community who participated by phone or on site for the fifteen different dialogues during 2000–2001. The expert community resources for the background materials—the transcriptions, bibliography, list of historic buildings, and chronologies—are available in written form on the website www.clevelandartists.org and helped complete the many components of the project.

Two special people helped the Cleveland Artists Foundation launch the Dialogue Series process. We dedicate our efforts to Foster Armstrong, professor of Architecture, Kent State University School of Architecture, CAF trustee; and Herbert Strawbridge, civic leader. Their voices were heard.

The Dialogue Series

A series of dialogues during 2000–2001 examined the creative essence of our region's visual arts through public discussions with experts on its development.

Topics and Speakers

"Our Regional Culture: Place, People, and Industry," June 6, 2000, Western Reserve Historical Society
Tim Donovan, director Ohio Canal Heritage Corridor; John Grabowski, director of research, Western Reserve Historical Society; John Nottingham, copresident, Nottingham-Spirk Design Inc.
Moderator: William Busta, gallery director and independent curator

"The Man-Made Environment: Architecture," September 19, 2000, Cleveland Restoration Society
Paul Volpe, AIA, City Architecture, Inc.; Robert Madison, FAIA, Robert P. Madison International, Inc.; Kathleen Crowther, executive director, Cleveland Restoration Society
Moderator: Ruth Durack, director, Cleveland Urban Design Collaborative
Resources: Michael Benjamin, AIA president, Cleveland chapter; Charles Adams, chair, Citywide Design Review Committee

"Museums, Libraries, and Other Collections," November 1, 2000, Cleveland Public Library
Andrew Venable, director, Cleveland Public Library; Stephen Sietz, head of Fine Arts and Special Collections, Cleveland Public Library; Katharine Lee Reid, director, Cleveland Museum of Art; Toby Devan Lewis, curator of corporate art, Progressive Insurance
Moderator: Nina Freedlander Gibans, cultural consultant
Resource: Kay Taber, art consultant

"Contemporary Art, the Museums and Galleries," January 30, 2001, Center for Contemporary Art
Jill Snyder, director, Cleveland Center for Contemporary Art (now Museum of Contemporary Art Cleveland); Mitchell Kahan, director, Akron Museum of Art; William Busta, independent curator; Susan Channing, director, SPACES

Moderator: Tom Hinson, curator of photography, Cleveland Museum of Art

"The Artist: Past and Present," March 20, 2001, Cleveland Institute of Art

Holly Morrison, artist; Don Harvey, artist; Michelangelo Lovelace, artist

Moderator: Frances Taft, professor of liberal arts, Cleveland Institute of Art

"Forging the Future," April 21, 2001, Cleveland Museum of Art

Keynote speaker: Susan Szenasy, editor, *Metropolis* magazine

Regional Art Trends, 1950–2000

Frances Taft, Cleveland Institute of Art, 1950–70; Tom Hinson, Cleveland Museum of Art, 1970–90; Barbara Tannenbaum, chief curator and curator of public programs, Akron Art Museum, 1980–2000

Moderator: Ken Emerick, Individual Artists/Media Art Coordinator, Ohio Arts Council

The Critic's View

David Kanzeg, 90.3WCPN/WVIZ/PBS ideastream, program director; Steven Litt, art and architecture critic, *Plain Dealer;* Kathleen Coakley, vice president, Malrite Corporation

Moderator: Dennis Dooley, senior editor, *Northern Ohio Live* magazine

Shoreby Club Discussion, March 1, 2001

Charles Sallee, artist; Peter van Dijk, architect, van Dijk, Westlake, Reed, Leskowsky, Architects; Richard Fleischman, architect, Richard Fleischman Architects, Inc.; Ernestine Brown, owner, Malcolm Brown Gallery; Dick Wootten, writer; James Mazurkewicz, master designer and craftsman, Potter and Mellen; Richard Moore, owner, Bonfoey Company

Moderator: Nina Freedlander Gibans, cultural consultant

Planning and Development

Artists Discussion, January 2000, the Sculpture Center

H. Carroll Cassill, David Davis, David Deming, Masumi Hayashi, Henry Halem, Michael Loderstedt, John Pearson, Gloria Plevin, Phyllis Sloane, Mark Soppeland

Advisory and Planning Sessions, January 2000

Carol Bosley, WVIZ/PBS ideastream; Robert Conrad, president, WCLV; Kristin Chambers, Cleveland Center for Contemporary Art; Joan Clark, Cleveland Public Library; Paul Gottlieb, Center for Regional Economic Studies, Case Western Reserve University; William A Gould, artist/architect; Gladys Haddad, professor, Case Western Reserve University; Richard Karberg, professor, Cuyahoga Community College; Geraldine Kiefer, assistant professor, Kent State University; Walter Leedy, professor, Cleveland State University; Norman Krumholz, professor, Cleveland State University; Hunter Morrison, then director of city planning, City of Cleveland; Leon Plevin, pesident, Cleveland Artists Foundation; Ann Olszewski, Preservation, Cleveland Public Library; William Robinson, Cleveland Museum of Art; Ted Sande, consultant; Marjorie Talalay, New Gallery (now Cleveland Center for Contemporary Art); Jane Tesso, curator, BP America.

Community Resources

Henry Adams, Case Western Reserve University; Diane Bell, Ann Caywood Brown, Kathleen Cerveny, Cleveland Foundation; Teresa DeChant, art consultant, Cleveland Clinic; Joellen deOreo, Cleveland Museum of Art; Susan dePasquale, Ohio Arts Council; Deena Epstein, the George Gund Foundation; Diane Hart, AIA Cleveland; Robert Gaede, FAIA, historic list of buildings; Bill Jirousek, the Sculpture Center; Brenda Kroos, Brenda Kroos Gallery; Robert Kurtz, Artists Archives of the Western Reserve; Rachel Nelson, chronology of highlights over the 100 years; Trudy Wiesenberger, art coordinator, University Hospitals; Richard Zellner; Susan Leggett, Cleveland Artist Foundation Trustee; John Chaich, Cleveland Center for Contemporary Art; Joellen DeOreo, Cleveland Museum of Art; Bill Kennedy, Cleveland Museum of Art; Kim Whitsett, Cleveland Restoration Society; David Williams, Cleveland Public Library; Marianne Berardi, director, Cleveland Artists Foundation; Martina Takac, administrative assistant, Cleveland Artists Foundation; Christopher Bedford, Education Outreach, Cleveland Artists Foundation; Christine Shearer, former director, Cleveland Artists Foundation.

Producers and Technical Support for the *Creative Essence* Video

WCPN/PBS ideastream: Al Dahlhausen, Jim Goulders, David Kanzeg

WVIZ/PBS ideastream: Carol Bosley, David Brodowsky, Linda Harris, Julie Henry, Dean Jordan, Jim Kolendo, Gary Manke, Mark Rosenberger, David Staurch

CINECRAFT Productions, Inc.: Jesse Epstein, Rachel Steinberg

Bibliographical Essay

The comprehensive histories of Cleveland usually start with William Ganson Rose, *Cleveland: The Making of a City* (Cleveland, 1950; reprint, Kent, Ohio: Kent State Univ. Press, 1990), followed by the *Encyclopedia of Cleveland History*, 2d ed. (Bloomington: Indiana Univ. Press, 1996). Other condensed histories that are instructive on Cleveland include Thomas F. Campbell and Edward M. Miggins, eds., *The Birth of Modern Cleveland, 1865–1930* (Cleveland: Western Reserve Historical Society, 1988), and David C. Sweet, with Katheryn Wertheim Hexter and David Beach, eds., *The New American City Faces Its Regional Future: A Cleveland Perspective.* (Athens: Ohio Univ. Press. 1999).

On Cleveland art there are a few books and many excellent written and photographic sources that can be found at the Cleveland Museum of Art, the Kent Smith Library at Case Western Reserve University, Cleveland State University, the Cleveland Institute of Art, the Western Reserve Historical Society, and the Archives of American Art at the Smithsonian Institution, Washington, D.C. There are complete bibliographical and chronological notes in William H. Robinson and David Steinberg, *Transformations in Cleveland's Art, 1796–1946: Community and Diversity in Early Modern America* (Cleveland: Cleveland Museum of Art, 1996), which is the most complete study of this region's art to date. One of the most useful resources is the state compendium *Artists in Ohio, 1787-1900: A Biographical Dictionary,* compiled and edited by Mary Sayre Haverstock, Jeannette Mahoney Vance, and Brian Meggitt (Kent, Ohio: Kent State Univ. Press, 2000). Elizabeth McClelland's collected articles on exhibits and artists (1970–90) in *Cleveland Writers on Cleveland Artists: An Anthology,* Cleveland Artists Series (Cleveland: John Carroll University, 1990)

establishes a solid base from which to examine the region's recent art.

Helpful resources on architecture are Robert C. Gaede and Robert Kalin, eds., *Guide to Cleveland Architecture,* 2d ed. (Cleveland: American Institute of Architects, 1997); Eric Johannesen, *A Cleveland Legacy: The Architecture of Walker and Weeks* (Kent, Ohio: Kent State Univ. Press, 1999) and *Cleveland Architecture 1876–1976* (Cleveland: Western Reserve Historical Society, 1979); and Mary-Peale Schofield, *Landmark Architecture of Cleveland* (Pittsburgh: Ober Park Associates, 1976).

Good background material on those who spearheaded the region's industrial and aesthetic development can be found in Ian Haberman, *The Van Sweringens of Cleveland: The Biography of an Empire* (Cleveland: Western Reserve Historical Society, 1979), and Leslie Piña, *Louis Rorimer* (Kent, Ohio: Kent State Univ. Press, 1990). Memoirs, interviews, and records add additional information and insight; the library at Cleveland City Hall is a useful repository.

Giving "region" a perspective and context helps consolidate issues. The approaches of William Gerdts's *Art Across America: Two Centuries of Regionalist Painting,* vols. 1–3 (New York: Abbeville Press, 1990); Stuart Plattner's *High Art Down Home: An Economic Ethnography of a Local Art Market* (Chicago: Univ. of Chicago Press, 1996); Chris Wilson's *The Myth of Santa Fe* (Albuqueque: Univ. of New Mexico Press, 1997); and Nina Gibans's *The Community Arts Council Movement: History, Opinions and Issues* (New York: Praeger, 1981) synthesize different general and particular arts histories and environments across the country. Robert Sterns, ed., *Illusions of Eden: Visions of the American Heartland,* Arts Midwest and the Ohio Arts Council's International Program, in partnership with the Columbus Museum of Art, catalog and exhibition (Columbus: Columbus Museum of Art, 2001), is a monumental attempt to define region.

Holly Rarick Witchey and John Vacha, *Fine Arts in Cleveland: An Illustrated History* (Bloomington: Indiana Univ. Press, 1994) gives a good overview of the cultural history and development of all of the arts of Cleveland. Mark Bassett and Victoria Naumann's *Cowan Pottery and the Cleveland School* (Atglen, Pa.: Schiffer, 1996) beautifully documents and illustrates the legacy of Cowan pottery here while laying the wider context for the work done here.

Books about individual regional artists usually accompany exhibits. Henry Adams, *Viktor Schreckengost and 20th Century Design,* catalog and exhibition (Cleveland: Cleveland Museum of Art, 2000), is by far the most comprehensive. Some single-artist catalogs focus our attention on particular aspects of their work. An example is William H. Robinson, *Clarence Carter: The Unknown Snapshot Studies, 1904–2000,* catalog and exhibition (Portsmouth: Southern Ohio Museum, 2004). Sometimes important insight is gained in the essays written for specific exhibits, such as Roger Welchan's catalog essay for the exhibit *David E. Davis: Transformations* (Youngstown, Ohio: Butler Institute of Art, 2000), or those written for exhibits at other area museums or galleries.

Other such catalog publications derive from the twenty years of the Cleveland Artists Foundation's research and include Henry Adams's *Paul Travis,* catalog (2000). The collective and selected publications from this organization's work provide the basis for much of the regional art research. The most important are: *August F. Biehle, Jr., Ohio Landscapes* (1986); *Harmonic Forms on the Edge: Geometric Abstraction in Cleveland; A Brush with Light: Watercolor Painters of Northeast Ohio, 1903–1958* (1998); *F. C. Gottwald and the Old Bohemians* (1993); *Henry Keller's Summer School in Berlin Heights,* artists include Henry Keller, Frank N. Wilcox, Grace Kelly, Clara Deike, August Biehle Jr. (1990); *Provocative Pens Four Cleveland Cartoonists* (1992); *Cosmic Rhythms: Athena Tacha's Public Sculpture* (1998); *Carl Gaertner: A Story of Earth and Steel* (2000). *Hungarians at the Easel* (2005). Contributing editors and writers to these catalogs include: Marianne Berardi, Ann Brown, Daniel H. Butts, Ruth Dancyger, Mary Sayre Haverstock. Edward B. Henning, Carolyn Jirousek, Ellen G. Landau, Elizabeth McClelland, Nannette V. Maciejunes, O. P. Reed Jr., William H. Robinson, Rotraud Sackerlotsky, and Christine Fowler Shearer.

The Cleveland Artists Foundation's Ohio Artists Now monograph series on individual artists are for some the most comprehensive study of their work. They include:

Daniel H. Butts III, *Phyllis Sloane* (1996); Ruth Dancyger, *Phyllis Seltzer* (1996); and Elizabeth McClelland, *Shirley Aley Campell* (1995), *Mary Lou Ferbert* (1993), *La Wilson* (1994), and *Gloria Plevin* (1998).

Sometimes publications have distilled the contributions of artists and are the only comprehensive summary of work, examples being Ruth Dancyger's work on *Edris Eckhardt, Cleveland Sculptor,* ed. Roger Welchans, Cleveland Artists Series (Cleveland: John Carroll University, 1990) and *Kubinyi and Hall,* Cleveland Artists Series (Cleveland: John Carroll University, 1988).

The regional crafts are perhaps less well documented. Two of the most important summary articles are William Baran-Mickle, "Frederick Miller: A Precarious Balance," *Metalsmith* (Spring 1993); and Deborah Krupenia, "John Paul Miller," *American Craft Magazine* (Dec. 2002/Jan. 2003).

Catalogs from museums outside of the region, such as *American Ceramic: The Collection of the Everson Museum of Art,* ed. Barbara Perry (New York: Rizzoli, 1989), are important to give context to the regional work.

Videotapes are another form of distilled information. Two such tapes are Helen Biehle, *European Vision, American Eye: The Life and Art of August F. Biehle Jr. 1885–1979,* 25-minute video (Cleveland: Cleveland Artists Foundation, 1990); and Nina Gibans, *Creative Essence 1900–2000,* 47-minute video (Cleveland: Cleveland Artists Foundation, 2003; DVD version included in this book).

The text of the following out-of-print Cleveland Artists Foundation symposia presentations are available at www.clevelandartandhistory.org: Mary Koster, Barbara Messner, and Sandy Reichert, eds., *Cleveland's Artistic Heritage,* proceedings of symposium, Cleveland Museum of Art, Mar. 1996 (Cleveland: Cleveland Artists Foundation, 1997); Sandy Reichert, ed., *Cleveland as a Center of Regional American Art,* proceedings, Cleveland Museum of Art, Nov. 13–14, 1993 (Cleveland: Cleveland Artists Foundation, 1993); *Yet Still We Rise: African American Art in Cleveland 1920–1970,* catalog and exhibition with essays by Alfred L. Bright, Samuel L. Black, and Pamela McKee (Cleveland: Cleveland Artists Foundation, 1996). The site also includes Karal Ann Marling's "New Deal Art in Cleveland," in *Federal Art in Cleveland* (Cleveland: Cleveland Public Library, 1974).

Important are books that give insight through the writings of the artists themselves, such as J. Benjamin Townsend, *Charles Burchfield Journals: The Poetry of Place* (Albany: SUNY Press, 1993), and Frank Nelson Wilcox, *Indian Trails,* ed. William McGill (1933; reprint, Kent, Ohio: Kent State Univ. Press, 1970), as well as his book on *The Ohio Canals,* ed. William McGill (Kent, Ohio: Kent State Univ. Press, 1969).

Individual chapters from books like Romare Bearden and Harry A. Henderson, *A History of African-American Artists from 1792 to the Present* (New York: Pantheon Books, 1993), provide insight as to a regional artist's reflection on his experience here, and inclusion in such a book is fundamental to recognition.

Most of the information about specific artwork and biographies of especially of living artists are found in the catalogs of exhibits that included works. The catalogs of the May Shows between 1919 and 1993 are now on the website of the Cleveland Museum of Art. Brochures, catalogs and individual artist websites are enormously helpful for expansion of biographies and careers of living artist. Catalogs organize our thinking about looking at art. Today, printed material is almost always available about exhibiting artists often accompanied by thoughtful essays in museums and galleries: *Walking Tour and Guide to Public Art in Downtown Cleveland* (Cleveland: Cleveland Public Art. 2003); Carolyn K. Carr, *Five Perspectives,* catalog and exhibition, artists Henry Halem, Patrick Kelly, Mayer, John Pearson, Judith Salomon (Akron, Ohio: Akron Art Museum, 1985); Michael Hall, "The Symphony and the Garage," in *The Spirit of Cleveland: Visual Arts Recipients of the Cleveland Arts Prize 1961–1995* (Cleveland: Cleveland Institute of Art, 1995); Tom Hinson, *The Invitational: Artists of Northeast Ohio: An Invitational Exhibition of the Works of Fifteen Artists* (including Christina de Paul, Kenneth Dingwall, Carl Floyd, Don Harvey, Masumi Hayashi, Curlee Raven Holten, Michael Loderstedt, Kirk Mangus, Richard Myers, Ken Nevadomi, Paul O'Keefe, Patricia Zinsmeister Parker, John Pearson, Annie Petres, La Wilson), catalog and exhibition (Cleveland: Cleveland Museum of Art, 1991); Hinson, *1994 Invitational: Artists of Northeast Ohio,* catalog and exhibition, artists Joan Damankos, Mark E. Howard, Eva Kwong, Craig Lucas, Christopher Pekoc, Audra Skoudas, Catherine Tigue, Lilian Tyrrell (Cleveland: Cleveland Museum of Art, 1994); Hinson, *Urban Evidence; Artists Reveal Cleveland*, Catalogs I and II for collaborative exhibition project sponsored by the Cleveland Center for Contemporary Art, the Cleveland Museum of Art, and SPACES, artists Judith Barry, Johnny Coleman, Christina de Paul, Kevin Jerome Everson, Don Harvey, Mark Howard, Ilya Kabakov, Joseph Kosuth, Michael Loderstedt, Tatsuo Miyahima, Holly Morrison, Paul O'Keeffe, Andres Serrano, Lorna Simpson, Brinsley Tyrrell, Lilian Tyrrell, Laila Voss (Cleveland: Cleveland Museum of Art, 1996); Jay Hoffman, Dee Driscole, and Mary Clare Zahler, *A Study in Regional Taste, The May Show 1919–1975,* artists Kenneth Bates, August Biehle, Shirley Aley Campbell, Carroll Cassill, John Clague, Edris Eckhardt, William McVey, Viktor Schreckengost, William Sommer, catalog and exhibition (Cleveland: Cleveland Museum of Art, 1977); Ohio Arts Council. *Transcending Traditions: Ohio Artists in Clay and Fiber,* catalog and exhibition (Columbus: Ohio Arts Council, 2000).

Institutional and artist websites have become a greater resource in recent years. See www.clevelandartandhistory .org for links and related information.

Index